MURDER

IN ROANOKE COUNTY

RACE AND JUSTICE
in the 1891 Susan Watkins Case

JOHN D. LONG

THE
History
PRESS

Published by The History Press
Charleston, SC
www.historypress.com

Copyright © 2019 by John D. Long
All rights reserved

Front cover: Map of Gum Springs. *From "Fort Lewis: A Community in Transition," Institute for Research in the Social Sciences, University of Virginia, 1930*; Watkins sketch. *Author's collection*; Roanoke County Courthouse. *Salem Historical Society*.
Back cover: Main Street. *Salem Historical Society*; *inset*: The three Webber brothers involved with the Watkins case. *Charlie Webber*.

First published 2019

Manufactured in the United States

ISBN 9781467144100

Library of Congress Control Number: 2019945084

DEDICATION

For Susan. We can never truly know you, and something tells me that is our loss. The historical record speaks clearly only of the last few days of your life. Beyond that, we know so little. What were your hopes and aspirations? When you were a little girl, what were your daydreams of tomorrow? However you pictured your future, dying in a cold Virginia mountain stream, victimized by your husband, abandoned by your family, surrounded by strangers, buried in a pauper's grave—this could not have been what you envisioned.

In life, you deserved better. In death, you deserved justice. And at the very least today, you deserve the dedication of the book that tells your story.

CONTENTS

"Something Like a Body in the Creek"

The springtime air was still too chilly to let yourself get wet, even mildly. At least if you wanted to remain comfortable. While a man worked in the April sunshine, he might generate enough heat to ward off the damp chill. But just sitting and riding, when every tree shook off a drizzle of raindrops, a body was bound to get cold.

Lawrence Anderson ducked to avoid a low-hanging branch, but a shower of drops fell down his neck anyway as the oxcart rolled down the muddy path. Though the day had gotten a little warmer, Lawrence's hours of toil had left him wet feet beneath his muddy shoes and trousers soaked almost to the knee. The spray of water from the branch caused him to shiver all the more.

Still, driving the oxcart of branches and "trash wood" down the mountain was so far the easiest part of his day. Soon after dawn, he had started the arduous task of plowing. April rains the night before had left the ground heavy, too stubborn to yield pliantly to the plowshare. But it was spring, and plowing had to be done. At fifteen, and with his father dead, Lawrence could no longer afford the luxury of sitting in the Gum Spring schoolhouse every day. The white children in Salem might stay in school a couple of more years and maybe even enroll at Roanoke College. But for Lawrence, no such opportunity existed. He was a man, and men worked.

The plowing for the day done, Lawrence had hitched up the ox to the cart and headed up the mountain to gather firewood. As often happened, some of the neighborhood boys rode along with him, not so much to help as to have something to do. Either too young for school or simply not made to go consistently, the younger boys tended to idolize Lawrence. The older boy didn't mind, though like many teenage males he was not entirely comfortable around children. But they had helped throw some dead branches in the back for him, shortening the time needed to fill the cart. With the brush wood leaving no room for passengers now, the boys ran ahead of him down the muddy mountain path.

As he headed shivering down Brush Mountain, he debated whether to unload the kindling at his mother's or grandmother's cabins or ride on toward Salem and sell the cartload for a little bit of spending money. If he drove on past the small community on the mountainside, in another half a mile he'd hit the macadamized road. He could stop at the farm of the great Captain Horner, who had helped hang John Brown so many years before. Or he could turn east and see if anyone wanted to pay a few cents for the wood. Maybe Mr. Chapman at Lake Spring Hotel would take the load—evenings were still cool enough that the guests needed fires in their rooms.

While mulling this prospect, almost half asleep with the swaying of the cart, Lawrence suddenly became aware that little George Law was saying something to him, or at least saying something in a singsong voice to no one in particular.

"They's a body in the crick, they's a body in the crick…" George seemed to be saying.

Lawrence pulled the reins to bring the ox to a halt and tried to figure out what little George meant, if anything. The barefoot boy, wearing nothing but a long gown that was caked with mud on the lower hem, pointed through the bushes to the creek, not easily visible from the path through the dense springtime vegetation, and ran away singing happily.

Lawrence felt a strange foreboding, a different kind of shiver. Something was wrong. He stood up in the wagon and peered through the scrubby trees but could see only occasional glimmers of the sun on the rapidly moving water. Heart pounding, he dismounted from the cart and walked up to where a break in the vegetation allowed access to the creek bed.

Sliding down the muddy slope to the creek's edge, Lawrence scanned downstream and saw nothing out of the ordinary. Maybe the Law boy had seen a deer drinking, or the body of a possum floating in the rain-swollen stream. Turning, he followed the creek's course upstream. Suddenly, fear gripped his stomach.

There, lying faceup in the water, was the body of a woman.

Lawrence felt paralyzed with fear. He knew he should move, should help the woman, should get help, should do something. But he remained frozen for what seemed an age. Eyes affixed on the body, his brain processed what he was seeing, the scene beginning to feel dizzily unreal to him. The woman was stuck on a little island in the stream, her dress hiked up, revealing her legs—in fact, the most Lawrence had ever seen of a woman's legs. She was one of his own race, a good bit older than he was, dressed in a fancy black coat and shoes much nicer than Lawrence typically saw in the Gum Spring community. He didn't recognize her, and he knew everybody in the small area.

One hand was trapped under her body; the other extended out from her side and seemed to be wrapped in a bandage or handkerchief. As he looked closely, a head wound became evident, blood still trickling into the creek's current.

Mouth dry, heart pounding, Lawrence wondered what to do. Should he wade out into the cold water and see if he could help the woman? Yet he still couldn't move. With a croaking voice, he called out, "Lady, do you need help?" As soon as he said it, he realized the futility of the question and felt silly for asking it. She was lying down in the cold water. No living person would lie motionless like that for so long. The woman had to be dead. Lawrence's head began to spin, and he briefly thought he might vomit.

Lawrence had seen a few dead bodies before, but always lying out in a neighbor's cabin or wrapped in a sheet getting buried at the Gum Spring Cemetery. Never had he seen a body like this, and he realized that she must have been the victim of foul play. He also suddenly realized one of his feet had been in the water for several minutes and was unbearably cold. Tearing his eyes away from the corpse in the water, he turned and scrambled up the muddy bank. Where to go? Straight to Salem to get Mr. Webber, the sheriff of Roanoke County? He was known to be a friend of the folks of Gum Spring and certainly should be informed—but at the same time, in the back of his head Lawrence wondered if he would be held accountable for the woman's death. He knew enough of the way the world around him worked. He knew it happened that black boys were often accused of crimes they didn't commit.

He could ride on home and pretend he never saw anything. He could fetch the Laws or their neighbor John Banks and report what little George had said but stay otherwise uninvolved. Or go down to the road and get Mr. Preston, who had been sheriff once and who would have some idea what to do. But climbing into the oxcart, he decided on another course. He would go tell his mother, Ann, and ask her advice in the surreal matter. His mother would know what to do. She always knew what to do.

He smacked the ox's flank with the leather crop and got him moving. Lawrence could not know that he was about to open up one of the most celebrated murder cases in the Roanoke Valley of Virginia; still less did he know that the deceased woman was in fact a relation—the legal wife of his cousin. He only knew that his mother would have an answer for him.[1]

THE BODY DISCOVERED BY Lawrence Anderson that April afternoon in 1891 was that of Susan Wilson Watkins, a recent resident of Milwaukee, Wisconsin. Although she had only been in Virginia for a couple of days and knew almost no one in the Roanoke Valley, it did not take long for authorities to uncover a reasonably plausible account of her last days on earth and to identify a suspect in her murder: her own husband, Charles Henry Watkins.

The resulting manhunt, trial and ultimate execution of Charles Watkins would be one of the most celebrated cases of the day and would attract national attention to the mountainside community of African Americans in Roanoke County. The public seemed to have followed the details of the case with attention comparable to the celebrated televised murder trials that have become a part of our modern culture today. It was a case that had everything to rivet the public: race, violence, bigamy, a fugitive manhunt, threats of lynch mobs, a disappearing witness, mistaken identities, a secret letter to unravel—suddenly and unexpectedly—the mysteries of the case. Few murder trials of the day could match the drama. And yet despite all of this, the case has been forgotten for decades.

I first discovered the Charles Watkins case accidentally, as so many historical discoveries are made. At the time I was the director of the Salem Museum in Salem, Virginia, and the de facto local historian for the town. One day, a friend asked who was the last person to be hanged judicially in Roanoke County; I replied that I had seen a reference to a "mulatto" who, involved with a German woman, murdered his wife and was given the death sentence for the crime. However, I said, I knew few other details and would see what I could discover. What I discovered was a treasure-trove of information and a compelling look into questions of race and justice in the post–Civil War South.

I confess that I began looking into the Watkins case with a bit of skepticism as to justice done. Here was a former slave, romantically involved with a white woman, accused of murdering his African American wife in order to continue the relationship. Surely, in a small rural county in the South there could have been little justice meted out in such a case. Endemic racism, the realities of segregation and the un-crossable barrier of miscegenation would cloud any attempt at a fair trial. If Watkins went to the gallows, he must have been railroaded.

But the evidence, I concluded, proved otherwise. Not only did Charles Watkins get a fair trial and a competent defense, but the ultimate verdict also was undoubtedly the correct one. The preponderance of evidence (circumstantial though it was) pointed solely to Watkins as his wife's murderer, and judge and jury came to the only possible decision. There could be no reasonable doubt about his guilt—there was no other plausible suspect. Besides, in the end he made a full confession, both in a letter that proved crucial to the prosecution and—if the contemporary newspaper accounts are to be believed—to authorities on the morning of his execution.

So this is not a case of justice derailed by prevailing racism. Rather, it is a case showing how the legal system could work, and even arrive at a proper decision, in spite of the racial attitudes of the day. By working as it should have, the case of Charles Watkins serves as an indictment of the many, many times justice did *not* triumph in the Jim Crow South.

Charles Watkins was born, lived, committed his crime and faced the consequences of it in a day when near universal racism prevailed. The predominant racial attitudes of Virginia in 1891—indeed of the entire nation—presupposed that the white man was superior, that people of African descent were generally suitable only for labor, that they were on average less intelligent, less trustworthy and had to be kept in their place. It was a deplorable world by modern standards. It was a world marked by injustice and prejudice and oppression. Decades would pass before much progress would be made in race relations.

But, shameful as that chapter in American history was, none of this made Charles Watkins innocent of the murder of his wife.

One need neither deny nor defend segregation and lurid lynch mobs to see that in this particular case, justice was done. Nor need one support the idea of capital punishment today to concede that it was the legally prescribed punishment in those days for a convicted murder.

There was no shortage, to be sure, of injustice in the South of 1891, but it was not a decisive factor in Judge Griffin's courtroom. That's not to say racial conventions of the day did not play any part in the hunt for, trial of and execution of Charles Watkins. No one can say that, by modern standards, racism was not nakedly obvious, especially in the paternalistic way the trial was covered by the media. Despite the injustices directed against blacks of the day, in this case there was a fair trial, and ultimately justice was done for Susan Wilson Watkins.

There is one conceivable area in which the court could be faulted in its quest for justice: discovering the role of Edith "Ida" Friebel, the white paramour of Watkins. Though early investigations assumed her to be an accessory either before or after the fact, she was not indicted, charged or even called as a witness. Although briefly arrested and held in custody, she was released and promptly disappeared, not to play any further part in the Roanoke County drama. Perhaps she proved to be an adept escape artist and all efforts to discover her responsibility in the crime proved futile. Or perhaps the white officers of the court were content to bring justice down on the black man in their custody, with little interest in what (if anything) his vanished white partner had done. In truth, we can now never know which is the better explanation. But if justice was left incomplete, it was in this area, as we shall see.

Susan Watkins died, alone and betrayed, in a cold stream in the mountains of Virginia. The community, barely knowing who she was, laid her to rest under its own soil, then did its best to bring her killer to justice. The people did so not primarily out of racial animus but because of a prevailing moral sense—an instinctive conviction that murder, no matter the color of the victim, must be punished. Then, the entire sordid story, the names of victim and perpetrator, the drama of the manhunt and trial, all faded into historical obscurity.

It is time to bring the Watkins case back to light. It is, after all, a fascinating saga, and exploring it reveals many tantalizing glimpses into life and justice in a small Virginia community of the day. By knowing this story, we know ourselves better.

A note on sources: By far the best source for uncovering the Watkins murder case of 1891 is the *Roanoke Times*, a large and respectable daily newspaper published in the thriving railroad boomtown. Many of the details of the case are recorded only there, the first and often sole draft of the history of the affair. However, nineteenth-century newspapers must always be read with a certain degree of caution. Newspapers, competing for customers and advertising dollars, were easily susceptible to the temptation of sensationalism, and seldom were they impartial in their presentation of a story. This doesn't automatically make what they reported factually incorrect, but it does necessitate some occasional skepticism. Certainly, newspapers of the day, reflecting the society in which they operated, reveal a large degree of racist sentiment, undeniable and unavoidable, to the modern reader.

Beyond the *Roanoke Times*, the smaller adjacent town of Salem had a weekly newspaper that survives in part for 1891. The *Salem Times-Register* also covered the Watkins case extensively and occasionally included details not covered by its bigger neighbor (though, of course, only once a week).

I have usually not provided endnotes for newspaper references, as any of the stories may be easily found in an issue of one or both papers immediately following the events in question. Should one wish to double check my research on a point that includes no citation, simply consult the appropriately dated newspapers. Digital images of the *Roanoke Times* may be seen through the Library of Congress website at chroniclingamerica.loc.gov or from the Library of Virginia website at virginiachronicle.com. The *Salem Times-Register* is available through the Virginia Chronicle project with some loose issues in the archives of the Salem Museum.

There are occasionally obvious errors and contradictions in the newspaper accounts—for instance, getting Susan Watkins's first name wrong in multiple stories. I have ignored or corrected these errors in my presentation as needed.

There is no official transcription of trial testimony from the case. Court records survive but generally deal tersely with the overall legal business of the court, not with such mundane business as transcribed witness statements. Therefore, the newspapers are the best source of what was said in the courtroom, usually in short synopsis only. Since they can't be challenged, I have taken them at face value. The handwritten records of the 1891 coroner's inquest survive, and these record the words of some participants. Both of these official records are to be found in the Library of Virginia in Richmond.

You will immediately note that each chapter begins with a fictionalized introduction, a first-person account featuring one of the characters related to the Watkins affair. These are intended to represent how certain actual players in the drama may have viewed the case at a particular point in time, as their lives intersected with it. These introductions are my invention, although they are based on the historical record. Obviously, the thoughts of such persons and most of the conversations are my extrapolations. It is my hope that these small tableaus will give you a sense of (as German historians might put it) "wie es eigentlich gewesen"—how it actually was.

1

"An Ill-Spent Life"

There used to be ghosts on this mountain, thought John Banks. Wonder where they went. Wonder if they'll come back.

He settled down against an old oak, wrapping a blanket around his shoulders against the chill. John had long ago gotten over his fear of haunts, and for years he had thought nothing of strolling through these woods in the dark. But sitting by the bank, keeping watch over a dead woman—that was enough to bring back to mind some of the spirits that he once felt lurking on shadowy mountainside.

He reflected again that he'd rather be at home. Of course, Sheriff Webber said he'd pay him and Sam Strickler $1.50 each to stand guard at the scene all night. A dollar and a half wasn't a lot, but John had earned less for much harder work.

Sam Strickler came into the circle of firelight with an armload of wood, silently. Sam never talked much. John didn't mind; there didn't seem to be much that needed to be said through the lonely, wakeful hours. Soon the fire was blazing again and they could smell the coffee brewing in the pot.

John glanced over at the woman, lying on the bank under a blanket. She was outside of the circle of firelight, but they'd placed a lantern nearby to keep nighttime critters at bay. By the time the sheriff had gotten out to Gum Spring to view the crime scene, it was too late in the day to bring a hearse out and take her to Oakey's in Salem.

Though he'd never been near a murder scene before, John understood the need for guards. It would be unseemly just to leave the woman unattended.

When a person died, the family sat up with him or her. This lady had no family in these parts, so he and Sam would act the part.

Besides, curious onlookers had already trampled over such evidence as footprints. Instinctively, John had paid close attention to details when he came to the spot in late afternoon, one of the first from the neighborhood. He'd noted the woman's position, a woman's and a man's tracks in the mud and that there was no sign that the woman had been dragged off of the creek bank. The sheriff appreciated these observations and let him know he'd need to relate them to the coroner's jury the next day.

Sam suddenly spoke. "You don't think Charlie would come back here, do you? Hoping to hide her better?" John hadn't considered that possibility. But after a few moments' reflection, he decided he didn't think it very likely and said so. John had known Charles for years and didn't think he'd return to Gum Spring, especially since pretty much everyone in the neighborhood already assumed that Charles had perpetrated the deed.

In fact, John knew he was gone from the area—he'd seen him heading away from the mountain as fast as he could. Just a few hours earlier, John had been returning home from work when he saw Charles and that strange German woman he called his wife. They were on the macadam road, and John stopped to speak to his old neighbor, a man he hadn't seen in weeks. But something was amiss, John could tell. Charles, usually so outgoing, barely mumbled a hello and rushed on. Of course, John couldn't imagine why at that point.

An owl hooted in the distance. The night was passing slowly and uneventfully, which was good. John stood and walked over to the shape under the blanket. If there were ghosts on the mountain, this Mrs. Watkins was now one of them. Her trials were over, ours go on, he thought, settling back down nearer the warmth of the fire.

NESTLED IN THE BLUE Ridge Mountains of southwest Virginia, the small town of Salem was a prosperous and pleasant community in 1891. It was a young town by Virginia standards—there were still folks alive who had known the earliest settlers in town, which dated back only to 1802.

That was the year a land speculator named James Simpson purchased thirty-one acres of land astride Virginia's Great Road, the main (but barely passable) thoroughfare for migrants heading west. Simpson platted out a town he named Salem, rightly assuming that westward traffic would bring opportunity. Within a couple of years, Simpson, likely under some cloud of financial distress, had sold his Virginia holdings and left the state.

The town he left behind began to thrive, aided especially by the arrival of an unexpected business concern. The Roanoke Navigation Company was organized in 1816 to make the Roanoke River a waterway out of the mountains for cargo boats—an idea more reflecting the poor quality of the roads in the area than the navigability of the local river. Nonetheless, the idea brought about a wave of growth for the little town, ensuring that it would survive its infancy.

With bateaux plying the river and constant traffic along the Great Road, Salem became a busy place. With so many travelers passing through town, taverns and hotels proliferated. One such was the Mermaid Tavern, operated by one Chilion White. No less a personage as Andrew Jackson is known to have stayed in the Mermaid (or Mairmaid, as Jackson spelled it in a letter mailed from Salem).

For the first thirty-six years of its existence, Salem was a town of Botetourt County, seated at Fincastle, some thirty miles away. As the population and prosperity of the Roanoke Valley increased, the residents felt increasingly estranged from the rest of the county and dissatisfied with the multiday trek it took to record a death or register a land sale in the courthouse. By 1838, the region had seceded from Botetourt County and formed a new county, named for the river running through the valley. Salem, the only sizable town in the area, was chosen as the county seat for Roanoke County.

Salem's newfound status helped attract more businesses to town and a small Lutheran academy, soon renamed Roanoke College. By 1852, the nation's wave of railroad expansion brought a rail line through Salem, spurring even more growth. No one could know that the railroad would soon make Salem a military target.

When the Civil War tore the nation in two, Roanoke County dutifully sent its sons into the Confederate service. Boys from the valley would fight in virtually all of the major engagements, but the war intruded into the county only twice. In December 1863, Union general William Averell raided the valley to cut the railroad lines. His men burned the depot, destroyed a mill, seized supplies from a government warehouse and tore up about fifteen miles of track around Salem. But harassed by the enemy, Averell retreated without taking time to do more damage to the town.

Six months later, in June 1864, Union forces were retreating, after being repulsed from an attack on nearby Lynchburg. Pursuing Confederates caught up with the rearguard of General David Hunter's force and fought a skirmish a few miles north of Salem. The Battle of Hanging Rock was the only combat in Roanoke County; while it counted as a Confederate victory, it was too small and too late in the war to be of much consequence. The end was in sight for the Confederacy.

The conclusion of the war meant a reunion of North and South; it also meant, of course, an end to slavery. While slavery in the mountains of Virginia had not been as intensive as on the large tobacco and cotton plantations elsewhere, it was still a significant force in Roanoke County. Some one-third of the population of the county was African American, and these newly emancipated men, women and children faced enormous challenges with the new reality, where the white majority was not eager to surrender its dominance.

Roanoke County's black people were beyond a doubt treated as second-class citizens. While race relations in rural western Virginia were arguably better than many other places in the South, there was no sense of egalitarianism, justice or fair play when it came to African Americans. The county's newspapers and opinion leaders expressed decidedly racist viewpoints; such concepts as equal opportunity in employment and color-blind court proceedings were generations away.

By the 1870s, nearly a third of landowners in Roanoke County were black, but the total assessed worth of their real estate amounted to only 1.3 percent of all property valued, and 0.73 percent of all land.[2] So some opportunity existed for advancement by African Americans, but it was decidedly muted by the realities of segregated society.

The result was a community divided by race in profound ways. African Americans lived in tight-knit communities scattered across the countryside. In Salem in 1868, some freed slaves purchased lots of land newly platted out from the estate of one of the larger antebellum land (and slave) owners, forming the genesis of the Government Hill neighborhood and the Water Street community. The latter soon became a sort of black Main Street, the center of African American life in Salem and western Roanoke County.

Away from town, small, cohesive black communities emerged with picturesque geographic names like Catt Hill, Big Hill, Twine Hollow or, most significantly for this story, Gum Spring. Here African Americans farmed and raised families, by necessity interacting with the white community in business and civic affairs. But seldom did whites venture into these isolated neighborhoods.

Perhaps inevitably, there developed a latent mistrust in the black community toward the whites who oppressed them. An example of this was seen in

1878 with the murder of one Peter Martin. An African American railroad worker from Salem, Martin was returning home from work on the night of September 19. Newspaper accounts note that Martin was intoxicated and belligerent and had been in a couple of fights earlier in the night. But he had calmed down a bit after 10:00 p.m., when he was struck on the head and killed. At the time, he was in public on the street and in plain view of forty or fifty witnesses, all African American.

The next day, authorities arrested one George Rively for the murder. E.M. Armstrong, the local justice of the peace, considered the evidence but soon dismissed the case and released Rively. Apparently, there were not enough witnesses willing to come forward to carry the case to trial.

A local paper, the *Conservative and Monitor*, found this "a wonderfully strange thing." The editors lamented that "a man could be dealt a death-blow in the midst of a crowd of some forty or fifty persons, yet no one know who did the mischief."

The paper further feared that such a miscarriage of justice would reflect badly in the community and called for the hiring of "a good detective."[3] But there was no discussion of why such a thing might happen, why members of the African American community might be hesitant to assist the legal authorities by cooperating with investigators.

But vestiges of just such an attitude may be observed in the Watkins case thirteen years later.

AFTER A PERIOD OF postwar depression, Roanoke County had begun to return to prosperity by the 1880s. In 1881, word was announced that a new railroad, eventually called the Norfolk and Western, was looking for a site to build a new depot, shops and a hotel. Whichever community was chosen would be guaranteed instant security and explosive growth. Salem, as the county seat and only sizable community, felt confident it would be selected. The midsized town began to plan the transition to big city.

But it was not to be. A much smaller village known as Big Lick, a few miles to the east, raised the necessary seed capital to bring the railroad there, shocking Salem and the other contenders. It was tiny Big Lick that would become the big city, changing its name to Roanoke City by 1882. New industries, hotels and business concerns followed the railroad to the boomtown—and so did the people. The population of the "Magic City" grew enormously: prior to the coming of the railroad, Big Lick's population was under seven hundred. By 1883, three thousand, mostly newcomers following the influx of jobs, called the new city of Roanoke home. With the arrival of the railroad, the population was exploding with job-seekers and country folk looking to make it big. City leaders would report in early 1884 that more than five thousand people called Roanoke home, thus making the town eligible for the coveted status of independent city from the state legislature.[4] The 1890 census counted over sixteen thousand residents of Roanoke. No city in the South came close to matching the explosive growth of Roanoke.

Across the valley, Salemites must have watched this with a sense of awe and perhaps envy. Nonetheless, Salem experienced its own explosion in size and territory. With proximity to the thriving businesses in Roanoke and the all-important rail lines, Salem's leaders sold the town to outside industry. A cadre of well-heeled investors formed land companies, purchased farm acreage adjacent to town and sold off tracts to businesses looking for the mixture of small town and big city that the Roanoke Valley provided. The "Great Land Boom" brought eager job seekers to Salem, and the little town's population swelled—not nearly as explosively as Roanoke's, but the number of Salemites nearly doubled between 1880 and 1890.

Salem's bustling Main Street, as viewed from the courthouse yard. Dillard's Drugstore is the building on the left. *Salem Historical Society.*

By 1891, the Great Land Boom was fizzling out. Some blamed a massive snowstorm in December 1890 that dumped an unprecedented three feet of snow on the valley, collapsing buildings and killing at least one person. More likely, however, downturns in the national economy were responsible for strangling the local boom.

Besides the two communities of Roanoke and Salem, there was a smaller town of Vinton established in 1884 east of Roanoke. Roanoke County was predominately rural, with some corners so remote that life seemed little changed since 1838. For Roanoke, Salem and Vinton, there was one modern innovation that interconnected them socially and economically: a streetcar line (often called the dummy) had been completed by 1890.

The pace of change was unprecedented, and it brought inevitable difficulties. With a booming population came social ills such as crime, poverty, prostitution, alcoholism and exploitive child labor. The new arrivals found themselves disdained by older families; the working classes felt animosity to and from the upper classes who employed them. But most strident were the divisions by race. African Americans remained an oppressed minority, and few saw much prospect for change in this. Few whites desired such a thing.

In Salem and the rural sections of the county, it could be said that race relations were far from ideal but generally peaceful; in Roanoke City, there was a racial dichotomy constantly simmering on the verge of explosion.

WHILE ROANOKE COUNTY CERTAINLY had its share of crime, unrest and violence, capital murder was a rare phenomenon. In fact, only two men had ever been judicially executed by Roanoke County courts. During the Civil War, a Confederate deserter by the name of James Stover was confronted by a patroller, John Peyton, in the Cave Spring area of the county. Stover shot Peyton and escaped, but he was caught a few days later and jailed. In August 1863, Stover was hanged just outside of Salem.

In 1879, a feud between mountain families led to the murder of one Zachary Hayes in the 12 O'Clock Knob section of Roanoke County, then a remote rural region. Marcus Hawley was arrested for the murder and found guilty; he was hanged behind the Roanoke County Courthouse in November 1880. Interestingly, Henry Webber, then a deputy sheriff and jailer for the county, assisted in the arrest of Hawley. Webber, it will be seen, also played a major role in the apprehension of Charles Watkins eleven years later.[5]

It was during the maelstrom of the Civil War, in 1863 or so, that a young slave boy, always referred to as "mulatto," was born in Salem on the Mermaid Hotel tract. His name was Charles Henry Watkins. He was born the human chattel of Nancy White, the widow of Chilion.

In the frustrating miasma that was slave recordkeeping, it is difficult to uncover much of Charles's early years. Even the names of his parents are unknown. It would be said many years later, when the name Charles Watkins became newsworthy and there was for the first time some curiosity about his biography, that his mother died when he was about two—about the time the war ended. But no record yet uncovered gives her name. Charles told a newspaper reporter in 1891 that both his parents had died when he was a boy, but he offered no names.

Since Charles was mulatto, generally described as particularly "light-skinned," it might be assumed that his mother was a slave and his father a white man whose name (if known at the time) cannot now be discovered. However, the possibility exists that Charles's father was an unnamed mixed-race slave. We can only speculate.

However, we might note that in 1937, in one of the few retrospective accounts of the Watkins case, Watts Dillard (a relative of Nancy White) recalled that Charles's father was a slave of Chilion White. However, this may be a simple error of memory made decades after the fact. Perhaps Dillard confused Charles's grandfather with his father. Again, the shadows of history prevent any certainty.

Tantalizing but inexact clues exist about Charles's mother. There exists in the Roanoke County Courthouse a list of names for Chilion and Nancy White's slaves in 1860, an inventory made as part of the settlement of Chilion's estate after his death in 1859.[6] It is in every way a product of its time. The slaves are listed only because they were property and had value—they were not persons, not individuals. Names and approximate ages are given, but the appraised value was the purpose of the register. Only first names are used, and only as a way to distinguish one slave from another, much as Chilion White might have named his mules. While an important historical source for our purposes, the inventory is a thoroughly dehumanizing document.

On the list are several women who would be old enough to become Charles's mother in three years or so. One might be his mother, but then it's entirely possible that her name is not on the inventory at all for some reason. There is a Sally (age eighteen), Sarah (seventeen), Polly (thirty-five), Sylvia (sixteen) or Ann (twenty), who had a two-month-old daughter named Mary.

All of these women were valued at between $700 and $1,000 in the cold calculus of slavery. A Grace is also listed, age twelve, but Nancy White would report the death of a slave by that name a few months later, so she could not be Charles's mother.

White's will left half of his "servants" to his wife "to dispose of as she will." No other explanation is given. The disposition of the other half of his slaves is unclear, although some other undescribed "property," perhaps including these slaves, was left to three local men.[7] During the Civil War, an accounting of slave owners shows Nancy White in possession of nine slaves, roughly half of what Chilion had once owned.[8]

Also noted on the 1860 slave inventory are the names Davy (age fifty, worth $750) and Maria (fifty-five, $500). While their ages don't match later census figures well, these two are good candidates to be David and Maria Watkins, the grandparents of Charles Watkins. A Taylor, age eight, is likely Taylor Watkins, the uncle of Charles who figures prominently in the murder case later. Ann, mentioned earlier with an infant daughter, could conceivably also be the future Ann Anderson, a daughter of David and Maria and the mother of Lawrence Anderson, the discoverer of the body of Susan Watkins in 1891.

If we do not know the name of his mother, we know her fate: she died while Charles was still an infant, according to 1891 accounts in the local press (the only sources we have on his background). At that time, Charles was taken in by his grandparents, presumably the David and Maria mentioned above. With the end of the war in 1865, of course, all of Nancy White's remaining slaves were emancipated, and the Watkins family apparently left the Mermaid tract to live and work for the widow Lucy Johnston, one and a half miles from Salem. That 1822 house, now called Preston Place, still stands, currently housing a charming tearoom. Of course, the Watkinses would have lived in a separate cabin on the property.

Sometime not long after, the Watkins family relocated again, to the farm of George William Zirkle, where they no doubt labored on the farm. Later accounts say that Charles was "about eleven" at the time, so this was circa 1874. It was about then that Charles Isaac Preston purchased the large brick house and fertile farm from the Widow Johnston, so perhaps the new owner evicted the Watkins family. Interestingly, Preston was a former sheriff of Roanoke County; Zirkle would assume that office in July 1891, in the midst of the search for the fugitive Charles Watkins.

Soon after going to work for George Zirkle, David was able to purchase from his employer nine and a half acres of land adjacent to the Zirkle

The Preston Place in the 1930s. Formerly, it was the Widow Johnston's home, where Charles Watkins lived as a boy. *Salem Historical Society.*

farm.[9] This tract was in the Gum Spring community of Roanoke County, a small string of homesteads populated by African Americans. Nearby was a small school, so the move to the Zirkle farm presented Charles with an important opportunity: some degree of education.

Later press accounts indicate that Zirkle and county school superintendent William W. Ballard took a liking to the young Charles, the fatherless boy whose mother was dead. Ballard, it was recorded, provided books to Charles so he could attend the Gum Spring School, within sight of his grandparents' cabin. We can surmise that Charles was an eager student who showed great promise, or Ballard would likely not have offered such largesse. Charles did not forget his benefactor, either, remarking years later that when he attended "school at Gum Spring... Superintendent Ballard bought my books." He added that "the white folks are really the only friends I have...whites have been my friends since I was a boy."

We don't know how many years Charles was able to attend the Gum Spring School, but it was enough to give him a chance at a better life. As an adult, Charles would be obviously literate, articulate, astute, instantly likable to most who met him. Many of these qualities no doubt were honed during these adolescent years at Gum Spring.

The support that Zirkle and Ballard would offer to the promising young Charles was not the last impact they would have on his life, and their favorable opinion of Charles would evidently change. Zirkle was the man who arrested Charles Watkins in the summer of 1891. Ballard was the prosecuting attorney who tried to send his former protégé to the gallows.

In the 1880 census of Roanoke County, Charles Watkins appears as an eighteen-year-old laborer living in the household of David and Maria Watkins. He would claim for himself in 1891 that he was a "self-made man and have worked hard on Mr. Zirkle's place and Col. [George] Hansbrough's place."

Also in the home of David and Maria was Taylor Watkins, listed as twenty. Assuming this is the Taylor Watkins who would later testify against his nephew, he should have been closer to thirty years old. Both men are listed as sons of David, although Charles was a grandson—an easy mistake for a census worker to make.

Rumors would later circulate that Charles had married while in Roanoke County and fathered a child. But the local press discounted such gossip, and no evidence of such a marriage has been found.

We can, of course, only make guesses about the personality of young Charles. But it seems clear that later in life he would exhibit a predilection for the good life of fancy hotels and linen tablecloths—albeit as servant, not client. Farming was hard work, and it was unlikely to lead to much advancement in life for Charles. The most he could hope was that someday he might, through years of sweat and backbreaking toil, purchase his own patch of land, which only meant more work. It's not hard, given what we know of Charles in coming years, to picture the young man wanting more—a softer life, a taste of elegance, clean shirts and clean fingernails, satisfied customers telling him what a good job he had done and slipping him a dime or a quarter. Taylor could stay and push a plow on David Watkins's small farm—Charles wanted more from life.

Accordingly, as a young man, Charles left Gum Spring. He seemed to have worked first at the picturesque Roanoke Red Sulphur Springs Hotel in nearby Catawba for a while; he would later say the first patrons on whom he waited were Judge Wingfield Griffin and his family. Judge Griffin would preside over Watkins's trial years later.

In 1883, it seems Charles moved to the thriving boomtown of Roanoke. It must have been an exhilarating place for a young man with ambition.

Roanoke Red Sulphur Springs Hotel in Catawba, Virginia, where Charles Watkins began his career in the hotel business. *Salem Historical Society.*

The suddenly (and in many cases only briefly) prosperous residents had disposable income and many needs—for housing, furniture, sustenance, entertainment. Shops, hotels, restaurants, bars and dozens of ancillary businesses were mushrooming in the young city.

One person seeking to boom along with the boomtown was an industrious hotel housekeeper from Salem by the name of Josephine Woltz. In her midthirties and unmarried, Woltz somehow scraped together enough money to leave her job at Salem's Lake Spring Hotel and open her own boardinghouse in Roanoke, where the thousands of job-seekers made a ready market for renters of rooms. Once established in Roanoke, Woltz would also become a socially conscious, community-minded leader in the burgeoning city—called in 1893 "at the front of all charitable efforts in Roanoke for ten years."[10]

Sometime around 1883, she agreed to hire Charles Watkins, about twenty, as a worker in her boardinghouse at Fourth Street and First Avenue in Roanoke. His exact duties were never described, but they certainly would have included cleaning, hauling, carrying luggage, tending fires, cooking and waiting tables—if Woltz's establishment was that fancy. Charles would later be called an "irrepressible bootblack," indicating another of his assigned tasks.

It was a good move for a former slave. Not many mixed-race orphans could hope to escape the backbreaking life of farming. But perhaps even that was not enough for Charles. He apparently wanted more than his due wages. Charles Watkins became a thief.

The exact nature of his crime, referred to later as "theft" and "housebreaking," is not clear. Whether Jo Woltz herself or one of her tenants was the victim is not clear, but it seems that Charles was immediately suspected. Prison, of course, could not have been his idea of the good life he sought. Given a choice between arrest and exile, he fled town, a fugitive from justice.

Charles ended up in Knoxville, Tennessee. What he did there and how long he stayed are details that do not survive, but his criminal career continued. He was soon wanted in Knoxville for forgery, though more detail than that—what he forged or for what reasons—does not emerge from later press synopses. Soon afterward, the town sergeant of Salem, Jacob B. Frier, received a telegram to arrest Charles if he appeared in his hometown, where presumably he was still wanted for the theft at the Woltz boardinghouse as well. However, Watkins was nowhere near Salem, it seems, for Frier to arrest. Nor was he apprehended in Knoxville, though he would later brag that he spoke with the officers searching for him while wearing a disguise. He had "cut off his short side beard and blacked his face" and departed without being recognized, he later boasted to a reporter. The officers suspected nothing.

Charles Watkins apparently could be, when he wanted, a master of disguise and could move about in a way calculated to make no one suspicious. On April 11, 1891, while Charles was newly a fugitive wanted for the murder of his wife, the *Roanoke Times* reported that he had told acquaintances that he "has no trouble in escaping when he wants to." Although the *Times* did not name the source of this information, and assuming it was an accurate report, it would indicate that Charles had, prior to Susan Watkins's death, bragged about his ability to elude the authorities. The *Times* added that "it is rumored that he has had occasion to escape from punishment for various crimes, though no definite information has been secured concerning any of his previous crimes."

Escaping the detection of law enforcement would prove a useful skill for Charles Watkins. It would serve him well, if only briefly, on future occasions.

It's difficult for residents of the digital world to appreciate how easily a person could disappear in the 1880s. There were no electronic records, no Social Security numbers, no fingerprinting or DNA evidence. Yet the railroads had made America a rapidly mobile society. A person who wanted to dissolve into thin air in one place could easily appear elsewhere under an untraceable assumed identity or even keep the same name with reasonable assurance that no one could uncover the truth. There is no way of knowing how often such things happened.

Resources to locate an escaped fugitive were limited and expensive. No police department would expend too much effort on apprehending a suspect wanted for a minor crime like Charles Watkins's forgery. When Charles left Knoxville, or Roanoke before that, he pretty much got away with his misdeeds.

So where did he go? A full itinerary of his wanderings is impossible to reconstruct, but by 1885 he appears again in the historical record in Louisville, Kentucky. We know this because it was here that Charles Henry Watkins publicly promised to love, cherish and protect a wife, forsaking all others until death do them part.

Charles, the charming fugitive, got married.

2

"WIFE NO. 1...WIFE NO. 2"

Millard Fillmore Huff gaveled the bidding to a close. "Sold, the gold ring, to Mr. Oliver, for five dollars and a quarter!" While Oliver moved forward to arrange payment, the crowd shuffled and murmured as usual, filling the vacuum between lots with chatter, waiting for the next item to be announced.

Huff knew his business, although auctioneering was more a sideline to his grocery store than his main income. The auction was going well. It wouldn't be the best he'd ever officiated, but far from the worst. All the items so far had sold for about as much as he'd reckoned, and he figured the proceeds from the contents of both trunks would land in the $150 range. No surprises so far. That was good enough for the auctioneer, but the spectators wanted to see the unexpected, the surprise item, the item that went for a dollar but was worth twenty or the piece of overestimated junk that went for $20 and wasn't worth two bits. None of that in these trunks, Huff knew.

The newspaper accounts and the endless gossip had raised expectations, after all. Everyone knew that Mrs. Watkins had arrived with two trunks packed with fancy clothes and expensive jewelry, more extravagant than one might expect from a hotel maid. And that only stirred up more gossip—why had she come to Virginia anyway? What was she hoping to find?

Huff looked out over the crowd as his assistant prepared the next lots for bidding—a few breast pins that wouldn't go for more than a dollar apiece, he guessed. Many of the folks were there for the spectacle, to see a murdered woman's leavings. Most weren't interested in bidding. The folks were about evenly divided between the races, and Huff mused, not for the first time, that a public auction was one of the few institutions in which the races mingled more or less equally. If a colored bidder happened to outbid his white neighbor, he took the prize home, no matter the shade of his skin.

Of course, that seldom happened. The whites generally had more money and would buy the more expensive jewelry. Huff himself had purchased a gold watch—inscribed with the name Susan Watkins—for a good price: $22.25. He'd sell it for a tidy profit.

He reached in his pocket and felt the watch, and his mind turned to the tragic end of the woman who had once carried it. There wasn't a happy ending to this story, Huff knew, even if some folks got a bargain or two in the bidding. He was an auctioneer, and most of his business was the result of some tragedy—a bankruptcy, a divorce, a sudden intestate death, even a murder, as today. It wasn't always a happy business to be in, but it was a necessary service. He put out of his mind, for the hundredth time, the unfairness of it all. He picked up his gavel, ready to start again.

THE BRIDE OF CHARLES Watkins was Susan Jane Wilson, an attractive single woman around a decade older than he. They were married in Louisville on June 27, 1885. The marriage was recorded a few weeks later on September 7 by Clerk of Court George Webb of Jefferson County, Kentucky. Despite later claims to the contrary, there can be no doubt that the marriage between Charles and Susan was legal and binding.

A reconstructed biography of Susan Wilson has proven elusive, primarily because her first and maiden names are such common ones. Lacking firm details such as a birthdate, birthplace and the names of her parents, and since she left no heirs to carry on the particulars of her memory, it seems unlikely more than the last few days of her life will ever be well known to posterity. Still, some details emerge from the testimonies and the press accounts of her husband's trial.

Several times, the newspapers referred to Susan as "coming from Chicago," but whether that indicates her hometown or the place where she her journey to Virginia is less clear. The papers probably meant the latter, as we know Charles abandoned her in Chicago, but it may well be that she was born there. Charles, on the other hand, would remark to a reporter from the Salem paper years later that Susan was "born in Georgia, and then moved to Kentucky, then to Cincinnati and then back to Kentucky." However, his statements at that point may not have been entirely reliable. He had every reason to conceal the truth by then, and in the same interview he said he had married Susan in 1887 or 1888—two to three years after the actual date.

If born in Georgia, and if older than Charles as usually described, it is possible she was also born a slave, although no record ever describes her as such.

Susan would reveal, during her brief stay in Salem at the home of Benjamin and Mary Wright, that she had a brother in Chicago who worked as a doorman at a museum and a sister there as well. She also indicated to Mary Wright that she was a member of a "Samaritan's Lodge Number 12" and a church. She indicated to Mary that she would like to leave her estate to these two organizations. This was an odd subject to bring into a conversation with a woman who was a total stranger an hour or two before. Perhaps it reveals some sense of foreboding on Susan's part.

Susan was usually described as seven to ten years older than Charles—hence born in the mid-1850s. The culture of the day being fixated on skin color, she was often termed a "dark mulatto"—in one case, her complexion was described as "gingerbread." She was always described as well-dressed, with a predilection for the finer things such as expensive jewelry and gold-plated umbrellas.

Beyond this, little can be ascertained. We do not know how she and Charles chanced to meet or what she was doing in Louisville. But it's not hard to imagine her taken by the dashing rogue, a man always described as handsome and charming. "She seemed devoted to him," wryly remarked the *Roanoke Times* several years later. Like all newlyweds, they certainly started their life together convinced that the best days were ahead and they would always be happy.

Sometime afterward, Mr. and Mrs. Watkins migrated to Milwaukee, Wisconsin, and took jobs at the elegant four-hundred-room Plankinton House Hotel. Opened in 1867, Plankinton House had a well-deserved reputation as one of the nicer hotels in the thriving city, and for both of them to land jobs there indicates that they were hard workers. Charles, we know, was employed as a waiter, and apparently excelled at it. At no point since he left the farm to take his first job at Jo Woltz's boardinghouse did Charles seem to find difficulty getting a job; once employed, he was often quickly promoted.

Susan, meanwhile, probably worked as a domestic at the hotel. The *Salem Times-Register* would later say of Susan that she was "an industrious woman

Plankinton Block.

The Plankinton House Hotel in Milwaukee. *Author's collection.*

and made excellent wages, most of which had been spent in paying bills contracted by Charles."

But the Watkinses' marriage was far from idyllic. Susan would tell the Wrights that at one point in their five years together, Charles left her for six months and that he also spent another six months sick in bed while Susan struggled to pay his medical bills. She showed the Wrights the invoices: $1.50 a day for his meals, $24 for six days of two-per-day physician's visits—all paid from her $75 per month salary. Somewhere along the way the couple took out a $5,000 life insurance policy on Susan, which Charles later tried to have her turn in for the cash value. Susan refused.

But these trying bouts of illness and petty squabbles over money paled in comparison to the direst threat to their marriage: Ida.

OF THE WOMEN IN Charles Watkins's life, much more information about Edith Friebel can be ascertained. Both because of her less-than-common name and the undeniable fact that the nineteenth-century historical record paid much more attention to a woman with white skin, Edith's biography is far easier to reconstruct than that of Susan Wilson Watkins or Charles's unnamed mother.

Edith, or Ida, or Eda, Friebel, or Friebals, or Freible, or any of a dozen other variations, was born in 1868 in or near Dodge County, Wisconsin. Her parents were German immigrants Henry and Walburga Groll Friebel, Catholics from Giesen in Saxony. Like many German families in the Midwest, the Friebels seemed to speak German primarily in the home, and Edith was raised bilingual. After at least some time in Milwaukee, the family settled by 1866 near Mayville, where Henry (Heinrich) opened a prosperous cooperage on Main Street. They would be called a "pioneer family" of the town—a house associated with the Friebels still stands in Mayville. By the 1880 Census, there would be nine children in the household: Louisa, John, Edward, Anna, Henrietta, Joseph, Henry and Elizabeth, in addition to Edith, or Ida, as she was usually called.

From an early age, Ida was employed as a domestic servant, and by 1890, she had migrated to Milwaukee and obtained work as a maid at the Plankinton House. Here she met the dashing Charles Watkins. Charles was older, handsome, debonair and must have seemed exotic to the country girl with a German accent. His attention flattered her. The fact that he was married seemed to bother Edith little, nor did the fact that he was "colored," according to the terminology of the day. Wisconsin was a long way from the Deep South, and German Americans were notably less concerned with race than other segments of nineteenth-century American society.

Still, Edith must have known that such a cross-race attraction was far from socially acceptable. By modern standards, even a cosmopolitan city like Milwaukee was tinged with endemic racism. By taking their relationship beyond that of cordial coworkers, Charles and Edith were crossing a number of boundaries.

Nonetheless, Charles "seduced her under promise of marriage, which promise was repeated again and again," according to a later press account of the relationship. "He was a nice-looking fellow," Ida would later tell a Roanoke reporter, and she didn't "think it any harm to live with him"— though she acknowledged that when she moved to the South she realized (with some understatement) that "a colored man was not so well thought of as in Wisconsin."

In the summer of 1890, Charles and Susan Watkins suddenly resigned from Plankinton House and relocated to Chicago. Why they made this decision is not and cannot be known. Still, it's not hard to imagine that Susan may have found out about Charles's dalliance with Ida and Ida's infatuation with her husband. Perhaps Susan demanded the couple leave to separate the paramours. If that was her intention, it did not work.

Ida soon followed Charles to Chicago.

Then, on July 15, 1890, Charles woke up and told Susan he was going to a barbershop for a shave. He did not return later that day. Or ever. Susan had been abandoned by her husband. And Edith Friebel began to use the last name Watkins.

CHARLES AND IDA HAD a thousand options of where to go to begin their new, illicit life together. But they chose to return to Roanoke County, perhaps hoping that Charles's extended family would provide some support structure for the couple to start life together. Still, it seems a choice fraught with problems. Presumably, Charles was still wanted for the theft at Jo Woltz's boardinghouse. But more importantly if a mixed-race relationship seemed unusual in Milwaukee or Chicago, in Virginia it was illegal.

The couple consistently claimed to be married when they arrived in Virginia—Ida would later claim that she could produce a marriage certificate, although she never did so. In fact, the two could not legally be married, even if they at some time stood before an officiant and repeated their vows. Charles had a living spouse and was not divorced, so a second marriage was illegitimate.

But even if Ida had been free to marry Charles, Virginia law prohibited it. Chapter CXCII of the 1873 Code of Virginia, paragraph 8, stipulated, "Any white person who shall intermarry with a negro shall be confined in jail not more than one year, and fined not exceeding one hundred dollars." Curiously, it would not be technically illegal for Charles to be married to Ida—merely the other way around.

But the fact that they were not legally married did not decriminalize the relationship: paragraph 7 of the same chapter banned "any persons, not married to each other, lewdly and lasciviously associat[ing] and cohabit[ing] together." The race of the offenders was irrelevant under this provision, and violations could lead to severe repercussions: "they shall be fined not less than fifty nor more than five hundred dollars; and upon a repetition of the offence and conviction thereof, they shall also be imprisoned in the county or corporation jail, at the discretion of the court, for not less than six nor more than twelve months." Whether they knew the details of these laws or not, Charles and Ida were running a real risk by merely crossing the border into Virginia.

And yet, surprisingly, there were no ramifications—at least none ever mentioned in the historical record. The previous allegations of theft against Charles were not pursued, but no reason for this was ever recorded. Perhaps Josephine Woltz, if she knew Charles was back in town, declined to press charges. Perhaps some statute of limitations had expired. Or perhaps the victim of the theft was a boarder at the house who had long since moved on. Whatever the reason, if Charles had indeed committed a crime seven years before, no one in 1890 seemed to care.

Nor did the interracial relationship seem to attract much undue attention. Charles and Ida associated—necessarily given the racial conventions of the day—primarily within the African American communities of the Roanoke Valley. They were welcomed by the extended Watkins family and had little difficulty finding housing in Roanoke's segregated neighborhoods. But even in the larger society they seemed to raise few eyebrows. They got jobs in prominent hotels; they seemed to ride streetcars and walk the streets of both Roanoke and Salem unmolested. Even the local newspapers, which hardly could be said to have been on Charles's side in his trial and were far from paragons of racial equanimity, took his unconventional "marriage" in stride.

It would be certainly naïve to assume the couple were uncritically accepted by all of their neighbors, but there seemed to be a surprising minimum of stigma, and no legal action was ever even hinted against them.

ARRIVING IN ROANOKE COUNTY in late July 1890, Charles and Ida first went to the home of his cousin Ben Wright, a blacksmith in Salem. Wright and Watkins had apparently been close in prior years, and the newcomers were welcomed to stay with the family for some three days, "sleeping together as man and wife," Wright would later recall. The Wrights were apparently unaware of Susan's existence.

It's unclear if the rest of Watkins family knew he had ever been married to anyone other than Ida. A neighbor of Maria Watkins, Mat Bailey, would testify in the coroner's inquest that Charles had written from Milwaukee to his grandmother that he had married, presumably meaning his marriage to Susan. Assuming Bailey's testimony was accurate, at least some of Charles's Virginia relations should have been aware of another Mrs. Charles Watkins somewhere.

After three days, the couple went to the four-room cabin of Maria Watkins at Gum Spring, the home in which Charles had grown up. Charles's uncle Taylor Watkins and his wife, Lucy, lived in the same house and apparently at times so did Lawrence Anderson, a grandson of Maria. Charles and Ida stayed there briefly but soon gained employment at nearby Lake Spring Hotel. Located on the macadamized road just outside of Salem where a natural spring fed a couple of man-made lakes, Lake Spring was an elegant summer resort for wealthy clients who favored the cooler air and healthy living of Virginia's mountains. In 1892, a disastrous fire would put the hotel out of business—today the site is one of Salem's most picturesque public parks. For the 1890 season, both Charles and Ida worked there happily.

Lake Spring Hotel in Salem, where Charles Watkins and Edith Friebel worked in 1890. *Salem Historical Society.*

When the season ended, Charles went to Roanoke City and got a job at the majestic Hotel Roanoke on the hill above the railroad depot. Roanoke boasted many hotels of various descriptions and reputations, but the Hotel Roanoke was the most glamorous. Charles, an experienced waiter who seemed to always leave an impression and give satisfaction to both employer and client, fit right in.

Ida, however, had a bout of some illness and was taken in again by the Watkins family in Gum Spring, staying there some weeks to recuperate. Charles remained in Roanoke at the hotel. If anyone found it odd that a white, German-speaking Catholic girl from Wisconsin was living on Brush Mountain with a family of former slaves, no record of it survives.

Charles would later claim that he'd been offered a position at the nearby Ponce de Leon Hotel in Roanoke but turned it down because it paid too little. If Ida was not working due to illness, money may well have been a concern. It does appear that he spent some time at the Ponce de Leon, since a letter on that hotel's stationery would be found in Susan's effects. But soon he left for the position of head waiter at the Hotel Felix, across Jefferson Street from Hotel Roanoke. This was a smaller hotel but still well regarded in town. It remained in operation until about 1917, when the building, by then called the Stratford, was purchased as office space by the N&W Railroad. It was demolished in 1930 to make way for the railroad's new office building on North Jefferson Street.

Eventually, Ida recuperated enough to rejoin Charles in Roanoke. The Felix apparently did not offer Charles housing, and so the couple, still masquerading as man and wife, took a room in a boardinghouse run by a Mrs. Sheppard not too far from the hotel. But not long afterward, they moved again, although Mrs. Sheppard remained a close enough friend for Ida to turn to her in the hour of need. The new home was a room in a boardinghouse on Sixth Avenue Northeast run by George Washington and his wife, Phyllis. Once more the couple set up housekeeping and settled in for a comfortable, contented life.

But instead, only two weeks later in April 1891, there was a knock at their door—a knock that perhaps meant that their world, their charade, was falling suddenly and irretrievably apart.

Or perhaps, as some would later allege, that knock meant something entirely different: that a diabolical plot was finally falling into place.

"At Last She Came on to Find Him"

L ord, let this not be true. And if it is, don't punish us for the sin of strangers under our roof."

Phyllis Washington paced the floor, wringing her hands, stopping every now and then at the foot of the stairs to listen intently. All she could hear were muffled voices and indistinct words, but she could tell there was tension in that room above her.

It started as such a quiet Sunday, she fretted. George, her husband, had gone to the church as he always did; she'd decided not to accompany him and get a few small tasks done. That was violating the Sabbath, she thought. Maybe that's why this disaster had come.

Of course, the visitors would have come whether she was in church or not, she realized. She hadn't paid much attention to the knock on the door half an hour before. But when her boy answered, she peeked at the hall to see who it was. She recognized Mr. Wright, the blacksmith from Salem, a casual acquaintance of her husband, and his teenaged daughter. She didn't know the well-dressed lady with them. But when they asked to go up to Mr. Watkins's room, she thought maybe it was a coworker from the Hotel Felix. She turned her attention back to her cleaning while the footsteps climbed the stairs.

Her boy returned and said something was wrong upstairs. Dropping her rag, Phyllis went to the bottom of the steps and listened intently. Voices were tense, words were hissed more than spoken. "I am the real Mrs. Watkins!" she heard.

A door closed. She quickly climbed the stairs and saw the blacksmith standing in the corridor looking uncomfortable. "Mr. Wright, what is the trouble?"

"Mrs. Washington, that woman who came with us is the true wife of Charles Watkins. She's come from Milwaukee to see him."

Phyllis thought she would drop through the floor. How could this be? What did it mean? One word immediately popped into her mind, *scandal*. The Washingtons had already taken a risk renting to a black man with a white wife. That was unusual, of course, to marry outside of your race. But to have two wives—that was just wrong. It was…she tried to think of the right word, a word so disgraceful that she'd seldom heard used. Bigamy. That was it.

She returned downstairs to think, trying to sort it all out in her mind. While she paced the kitchen, she heard Wright, his daughter and the white woman Ida come downstairs and leave the house.

A moment later, Charles appeared on the stairs. "Mr. Watkins," she demanded, "who is that woman?" "She's my cousin," he replied. "She's all right."

"Ben Wright says she's your wife."

"Well, I'll make Ben tell a different story when he comes back. You don't worry about this."

"I won't tolerate this," she replied. "You will have to leave if any of this is true. A man can't have two wives."

Charles said again there was nothing to worry about, but the stricken look on his face was more believable. He quickly turned and left the house.

Phyllis wrung her hands again and returned to pacing, muttering her prayer of deliverance. Since she and George had moved to the booming railroad town of Roanoke and bought the house on Sixth Avenue, they had operated a reputable boardinghouse. They turned away heavy drinkers and men who seemed shiftless. But when the dashing Charles Watkins came to inquire about a room, they should have asked a few more questions. The white woman with a German accent was his wife, he said. They'd been married in Chicago where such things were not uncommon, he claimed. Although such a mixed marriage was highly unusual in Virginia, the Washingtons decided to allow the couple to move in. For the two weeks they'd been there, Ida had mostly kept to the room, but she was friendly enough when they saw her. She didn't seem to share the innate sense of superiority most white folks had. She had even given George a photograph of herself, which Phyllis thought odd.

Now, there was the suddenly revealed possibility that the two were living in sin the whole time. That was scandalous. It was even illegal. Although the landlords could claim ignorance, it might still reflect poorly on them, Phyllis feared.

The opening of the front door disturbed her troubled thoughts. Looking up, she saw George come in with a worried expression. "I passed Mr. Watkins on the street. He said there's a lady here claiming to be his lawful wife. Lord, what are we to think?"

Phyllis knew her husband was guileless, like the president for whom he was named. George could never tell a lie or misrepresent himself, and as a result, he could not fathom other people doing such things. He was too trusting sometimes, not a trait that Phyllis was quick to share.

"Ben Wright brought her here. He says she is the true Mrs. Watkins and not Ida."

"Charlie said otherwise. He said he took up with her a few years ago out west, but they aren't married. Lord, what are we to think? How are we supposed to sort this out?"

Phyllis had no answer. But a minute or two later, she announced her decision, and George knew, from years of experience, that it was an irrevocable one. "Well, they have to leave our house. That's all there is to it. Whether or not that woman is his wife, I think they are disreputable people, and I won't have them under our roof."

George shook his head and said again, "Lord, what are we to think?"

They were silent another minute more before Phyllis made another pronouncement. "And another thing. I'm going to charge him for the full month's rent."[11]

THE PASSENGER TRAIN CHUFFED steadily eastward down the track, carrying Susan Watkins to Virginia. To her estranged husband. To her destiny.

As she looked out the window at the countryside rolling past, she would see the flat land of the Midwest start to give way to foothills and then the mountains of the East. As far as we can know, it would have been the farthest she had ever ventured. Travel, then and now, can be grueling but exciting, yet for a woman in Susan's situation it couldn't have been an easy journey. We can only speculate about her state of mind, of course. What did she feel as the train jostled her mile after mile? Apprehension? Anger? Or did her heart beat a little faster at the thought that she may be able to reclaim the husband who had abandoned her the summer prior, a man she had once, and perhaps still, loved desperately?

Roanoke's passenger depot. The Hotel Roanoke is in the upper right corner; just to the left, partially hidden by a tree, is the Hotel Felix. *Virginia Room, Roanoke City Public Library.*

And what of Ida, the white paramour who had followed her and Charles to Chicago and then stolen him away? Would there be a confrontation? Did Susan relish the idea of a confrontation? Or did she dread the possible humiliation if, after she crossed half a continent to see him, he again chose the other woman over his lawful wife?

She couldn't know what awaited her in Virginia, and her concerns may have gone beyond the sort of reception her estranged husband would give her. Susan must have known that in a former slave state like Virginia, more so than in Chicago or Milwaukee, a person of color would face unpleasant realities and a depth of racism she had never experienced—or, if she was a native of Georgia, had not endured since girlhood.

But little could she imagine that the greatest threat she would face in those mysterious Blue Ridge Mountains would come from the very man she was going to see.

WHY WAS SUSAN GOING to Virginia? What did she hope to accomplish there? Did she intend to reconcile with Charles or confront him about his abandonment?

More importantly, did she decide to travel to Virginia on her own, or was she invited?

No indisputable evidence survives about the motivation for Susan to travel cross country in April 1891. But the little bit we do know raises some tantalizing questions. For instance, it seems clear that despite being estranged and living several states apart, Charles and Susan were not incommunicado. Ben Wright, Charles's cousin who was the first person contacted by Susan in

Virginia, would later say that she showed him a postcard Charles had sent her, and Ben's wife, Mary Wright, spoke of a "pile of letters." News accounts confirmed the presence of such letters—some "quite vulgar"—in Susan's trunks, but the contents were not otherwise disclosed.

But perhaps most compelling is the assertion made by Sheriff George Zirkle to a newspaper reporter in Wilmington, North Carolina, in July 1891. Zirkle, who had been investigating the case for some weeks at that point, and who certainly was privy to undisclosed information, told the reporter that Charles had written to Susan with the claim that his grandfather had died and had left him a "fine plantation." Charles had, Zirkle alleged, lured Susan to Virginia with the promise of a reconciliation and an easy life but with far more nefarious intentions.

Months later, the *Roanoke Times* would make the same lurid charge: that Charles had told Susan that he owned thirty acres and a house and that a diligent hotel worker like Susan could easily find work in the Roanoke area—lighter work at higher pay. But these claims were only "a tissue of lies, fabricated to lure the poor, simple woman to her doom, in order that he might enjoy the company of his white wife without interruption."[12]

There is another bit of circumstantial evidence to consider. On April 11, in a wide-ranging report on the progress in the Watkins case, the *Roanoke Times* included a brief intriguing account of a supposedly misdirected letter. It seems that a white resident of Roanoke by the name of C.W. Watkins had, some days before, received a letter addressed to a C. Watkins and signed "Susie." It was dated March 9 and mailed from Milwaukee. Noting that the spelling and grammar were bad, the letter, said the report, "upbraided Watkins for not writing to Susie, and the writer said she had not heard from Watkins since December, 1890." Mr. Watkins apparently set the letter aside and only thought of it again when the names of Charles and Susan Watkins became the talk of the town.

Nothing else about this episode was ever reported, so it leaves many questions unanswered. The whole thing could have been a hoax or a strange coincidence, but assuming the story and Mr. Watkins's interpretation of it to be correct, it would indicate that all communication between the two had ended three or four months prior to Susan's trip to Virginia. It also would establish that after being abandoned by her husband in Chicago, Susan returned for at least a while to Milwaukee.

So did Charles lure his wife across the country to her doom? No testimony of this sort of conspiracy was ever introduced in Charles's trial. The prosecution presumably must have been in possession of the letters Susan brought with her yet chose not to utilize them as evidence. Perhaps the lawyers did not believe the correspondence necessary for proving the prosecution's case. It should also be noted that when Susan arrived at Charles's door, her estranged husband looked shocked—and uncharacteristically flummoxed—to see her. It was arguably not the reaction of a man who had been trying to lure his wife to her doom.

Susan, of course, left behind no memoir to explain her expectations as to what she would find in Virginia. Removed by more than a century, we can only speculate. But there is one final bit of evidence that may help reconstruct her frame of mind: what she carried on her trek east. There is a surprisingly thorough inventory of her possessions in the Roanoke County Courthouse.

Six months after the death of Susan Wilson Watkins, the county staged a sale of the "goods and chattels" that she left behind. There was no known next-of-kin to claim her assets or help handle the estate (except her husband, then awaiting trial for her murder). The county had presumably paid for her burial, and as was the accepted practice in such cases, her possessions were auctioned off, with the proceeds going into the county's coffers to offset taxpayer expenses. As a result, a "list of personal property of Susan Watkins, deceased" was compiled by Sheriff Zirkle and dutifully appraised by appointed commissioners.[13]

The items, contained in two trunks she left behind, consist of the sort of things you'd expect a woman traveling alone across country to have with her: clothing, shoes, jewelry. But other items suggest more than a brief visit. She brought books, photographs, silverware, aprons, towels, sheets, a quilt and, interestingly, a guitar. In other words, likely all of her worldly possessions were on that eastbound train.

The inventory does not suggest a person who intended to return to Chicago or Milwaukee. It is possible that she no longer had a residence there where she could safely leave her possessions and was forced by circumstances to bring them with her. But it is easier to imagine, given the quantity and sort of items she dragged halfway across the continent, that Susan Watkins considered herself as making a permanent move to Virginia. And perhaps indeed it was in response to the invitation of her estranged husband, Charles.

WE KNOW MORE OF the first day or so that Susan spent in the Roanoke Valley than the entirety of the rest of her life. Inquests into the crime and testimonies from the trial, as well as lurid press accounts, record a sometimes surprising level of detail, even snatches of conversation. It is, sadly, a glimpse into the last hours of a woman whose life was rapidly unraveling.

It's not clear what time Susan arrived at the depot in the clamorous railroad town of Roanoke, but from the start nothing transpired as she must have envisioned it. At Natural Bridge, Virginia, about forty miles from her destination, she had sent Charles a telegram announcing her impending arrival and asking him to meet her at the station. He never received the telegram, for reasons never made clear.

Now, she must have stood on the platform, her two trunks at her feet, looking for the husband she hadn't seen in months. Minutes turned into an hour, maybe two. Susan knew no one in town and had no idea where to find her husband. He had written to her from the Hotel Roanoke when he worked there; it was in sight of the depot. Leaving her trunks in storage at the depot, perhaps she asked for him at the Hotel Roanoke. She could only have approached the black workers through a service entrance—marching to the main office and asking the white management would not have been an option for her.

If she did go there, she would have been told that he was no longer employed at Hotel Roanoke. He had, in fact, been hired at the nearby Hotel Felix, a smaller but respectable establishment just across Jefferson Street from the Roanoke. But Susan apparently did not know where he was currently working. She had also received a letter from Charles from the Ponce de Leon, another hotel in downtown Roanoke, although it is not clear if Charles had ever worked there. That establishment was a few blocks away—perhaps she tried to locate him there also.

As the afternoon wore on, she had no leads on her husband's whereabouts. She was alone and a long way from home.

But Susan was also resourceful and determined. She could have searched out a hotel or boardinghouse for African Americans to spend the night, but a young woman traveling alone—with a good bit of cash and some expensive jewelry—had to be careful. Some of these establishments would have a rough reputation, and she couldn't know which was safe for a woman in her situation.

But searching her mind, she recalled the name of a relation of Charles's, a man named Ben Wright who was a blacksmith in the county seat of Salem. With nowhere else to go, she left her trunks back at the passenger depot, took her pocketbook and a small satchel and caught a street car to Salem.

Salem was a much smaller town than the boisterous Roanoke, the type of quiet community where everyone knew everyone. It wouldn't

Hotel Roanoke, about 1889. Charles Watkins worked here for some months in 1890 and 1891. *Virginia Room, Roanoke City Public Library.*

have taken long to find someone who could tell her where the Wrights lived. And so she found herself knocking on the door of her cousin by marriage—a man who seemingly didn't even know she existed until she appeared on his front porch.

Benjamin and Mary Wright and their houseful of children lived in Salem, where he seemed to be a respected blacksmith, well known to the community. He would be described in the local press, with not a little paternalism, as "well-spoken," "well to do" and "quite intelligent." Returning home from work on the evening of April 4, 1891, Benjamin found Susan Watkins in his house, telling a story that must have baffled him.

The meeting must have been an awkward one, to say the least. As far as Wright knew, Charles was married to Ida. The couple had even stayed at his house ("living as man and wife") for a few days when they first arrived in Virginia the previous summer. So who was this stranger claiming to be his wife? Did she have the wrong man? Was she trying to extort money? Or was she telling the truth? Much of her story would have seemed plausible.

Susan did her best to explain herself and establish her credibility. In her trunks, still at the depot in Roanoke, she said she had their framed marriage certificate. But until she returned to get her luggage, she had with her some documents that tied her to Charles: receipts for things she had purchased for him in Chicago, a postcard he had written to her from the Ponce de Leon Hotel in Roanoke.

Interestingly, Benjamin would testify a few days later to the coroner's jury that he recognized Charles's handwriting on the postcard. At the time, he had no reason to suspect that his ability to recognize his cousin's penmanship would ever be called into question, as indeed it would be, months later at Charles's trial. That he claimed to be able to identify Charles's writing months before the trial certainly lends credence to this assertion.

Soon, Benjamin and Mary must have been convinced that Susan was, in fact, Mrs. Charles Watkins. They invited her to stay the night—what else could they do?—and Benjamin promised to take her to Roanoke in the morning.

That night could have only been an interesting one. According to the testimony of the Wrights, they must have had extensive conversation before calling it a night. Although they only ever spent one evening and one morning together, the Wrights got to know this sojourner from the Midwest fairly well. Susan told the couple about her family—a brother in Chicago who worked as a doorkeeper at a museum and a sister there also. She told Mary that she was a member of Samaritan's Lodge No. 12; she described a period when Charles was sick and she paid for his upkeep out of her seventy-five-dollar monthly salary. Ben learned the circumstances of Charles's abandonment of his wife and probably became well acquainted with Susan's opinion of Ida Friebel.

Interestingly, perhaps presciently, she also told the Wrights that she intended to leave any money she had to her church and lodge and that she had a $5,000 life insurance policy that Charles had once tried to cash in for his own benefit. Later press reports would indicate that policy had lapsed due to nonpayment of the premiums, however—if this was true, perhaps Susan was unaware of this fact.

These last bits of information seem out of place—not the sort of personal info one would usually impart to total strangers. Did Susan have some reason to fear her death could be imminent?

It's tempting to wonder what Susan's thoughts were as she drifted off that night in a spare bed at the Wright home. Here she was half a continent away from home, in the comfortable house of a happily married couple with a flock of children. If she had come to Virginia hoping to reconcile with Charles, perhaps this was the sort of life she hoped to find.

THE NEXT MORNING, BENJAMIN Wright, his eldest daughter, Laura,[14] and Susan Watkins boarded the 11:00 a.m. streetcar from Salem to Roanoke. The trip took about forty minutes, during which they may have conversed more, or they may have remained silent, wondering what was waiting at the end of that track.

Arriving in Roanoke, they went first to the boardinghouse where, as far as Ben knew, Charles and Ida were living. It was a Mrs. Sheppard's, in the vicinity of Hotel Roanoke. Ben took her there and then took his leave, no doubt hoping to extricate himself from the mess his cousin had made. Ben turned and made his way back down the street.

He hadn't gotten far when he heard Susan calling him back. Charles had moved from Mrs. Sheppard's to Sixth Avenue Northeast, to another boardinghouse Wright called "Brother Washington's." Resignedly, the party headed in that direction.

The home of George and Phyllis Washington was only a few blocks away, in a crowded neighborhood in northeast Roanoke that was a center of the city's African American life. The thriving neighborhood would be virtually obliterated as "blight" in the 1970s under the banner of Roanoke City's "urban renewal" efforts. In place of the homes, businesses and churches of Northeast, the city's main post office, civic center and other projects would be built. Older members of Roanoke's black community still bitterly recall the process not as "urban renewal" but as "Negro removal."

WHAT HAPPENED AT THE Washingtons' that morning in 1891 is well attested, between the testimonies given to the coroner's inquest a few days later and the evidence presented in the trial the following November. Although the exact order of events is not always perfectly clear, the following seems a reasonable harmonization of the various versions.

Locating the Washington house, the trio knocked on the door, which was answered by a young boy, apparently the Washingtons' son. He obligingly took the three upstairs to the room shared by Charles Watkins and Ida Friebel. Ben knocked.

It was Charles who answered the door. Seeing his cousin, he exclaimed, "Ben, I'm glad to see you!" Wright's daughter Laura pushed past him into the room, and it must have been then that Charles saw Susan. Wright would later testify that Charles looked exceedingly surprised. He had been washing when they knocked, and the morning was chilly. Charles seemed to start shivering when he saw his wife.

Meanwhile, the daughter returned to the corridor, bringing Ida Friebel with her. Susan looked at her rival contemptuously and grabbed her by the arm. "What do you call yourself?" she asked. Ida straightened herself and replied with two defiant words: "Mrs. Watkins."

"I am the real Mrs. Watkins!" retorted Susan, pushing Ida into the room. Laura followed them. Charles, more than a little nonplussed at this sudden and decidedly disagreeable visitor, turned to go into the room as well. Susan, understandably agitated, asked Charles why he had not met her at the depot the day before in response to the telegram she had sent from Natural Bridge. Charles responded that he had heard nothing from her. If indeed he had in the past attempted to lure Susan to Roanoke, he didn't seem to have expected her to show up that Sunday morning.

No doubt Charles's mind was whirling, trying to process what this unexpected turn of events meant. He turned back to Ben and asked him to wait. Perhaps he hoped his cousin would take Susan back the way they had come. He also asked him not to say anything to anyone—"I'll fix it all." Exactly how he could "fix" such a situation was unclear.

It may have been at this point—Wright's testimony is not entirely clear as to the order of events—that Susan turned to Charles and asked point-blank, "Who do you say I am?" Charles, no doubt crestfallen, confessed the truth: "I say you are my wife." The door closed.

Ben had no intention of waiting around in such an uncomfortable environment. But before he could leave, Mrs. Washington came up the steps to check on her mother, who apparently occupied one of the rooms. She'd no doubt also been alerted by her son that something odd was happening upstairs. The Washingtons and Benjamin Wright seemed to be acquainted, and in the hallway he told Phyllis the truth as he knew it: that the woman who had come to call was Charles's legitimate wife.

After about ten minutes, Ida and Laura Wright came out of the room and left the house, Ben Wright following. The trio went to Hotel Felix, and Wright left his daughter and Ida there while he went to "Nick Lewis'" for the rest of the afternoon. Perhaps this was a nearby bar—a Nick Lewis appears in the 1880 census as an African American barkeeper. It is unclear what Ida did for the afternoon or for the next twenty-four hours, but she was certainly glad not to be back at the boardinghouse.

Neither is exactly what transpired between Susan and Charles in his rented room known. But soon afterward, Charles went downstairs to exit the house, leaving Susan alone upstairs. Phyllis Washington met him and confronted him: "Mr. Watkins, what is the trouble?"

Jefferson Street in Roanoke, looking south. The wall of the Hotel Roanoke's western lawn is on the left; the Hotel Felix is just beyond the Stone Printing building. *Historical Society of Western Virginia.*

Charles had a quick fib at his disposal. "Oh, that lady is my cousin," he said, downplaying the situation. "She's all right."

Mrs. Washington wasn't buying it, however. "Ben Wright says she's your wife, and if that's so, you must move from here," she insisted. She would have no bigamists under her roof.

Charles insisted that he would make Ben "tell a different tale when he returned" and left the house. He hadn't gone far before he met George Washington, who presumably knew nothing of the recent happenings in his house, coming back from church. He confessed to his landlord that there had been a "fracas" at the house that morning. A woman had arrived "confessing that Charles was her lawfully married husband." In fact, Charles said—apparently forgetting the version he had told Mrs. Washington only minutes before—she was "only a woman with whom he had lived for about four years." Pondering this, Washington said, "If that's so, she ought not to claim you as her husband." He asked if the visitor was Charles's wife, and Charles denied it— "just a woman I took up with."

Washington replied, "I thought you was a respectable man and that yellow woman your wife." This statement, in the records of the coroner's inquest, is the only time Ida Friebel is described as anything except white or German. Perhaps she was dark-complexioned enough that she could appear mixed-race—yellow being a contemporary euphemism for mulatto. Perhaps this explains why the Washingtons were willing to rent a room to the unconventional couple and why Charles and Friebel raised so few eyebrows in segregated Roanoke. Or perhaps Washington intended it as a reference to Susan: We thought you were respectable, but now we find out that "that yellow woman" who just arrived is actually your wife.

At any rate, Washington gave Charles the same ultimatum his wife had: "You will have to get out."

Washington returned home and confronted Susan: was Charles Watkins her husband? His testimony does not record her answer, but of course it would have been in the affirmative. George told her she would have to leave. But Susan, seeking an ally, asked Phyllis for permission to stay until Charles returned. She had nowhere else to go.

The record is silent about the next few hours. Susan was at the Washingtons' by herself, it seems. It could hardly have been how she had envisioned the afternoon going. At some point, she told Phyllis that Charles had asked her to accompany her in a buggy to his grandmother's house on Brush Mountain, and she had declined. Nothing further was said by Mrs. Washington about this assertion, but it is an interesting one. Did Susan sense that such a journey would be dangerous?

Charles, according to Ben Wright's trial testimony, had gone to the Felix, although whether he was working or merely whiling away the time is not clear. Ida had gone there earlier; perhaps the two conferred. It is also not known where Ida spent the night. Perhaps she went to Mrs. Sheppard, her former landlady, who appeared to be a personal friend, as we will see.

About 6:20 p.m. or so, Benjamin Wright testified that he returned to the Washingtons' home, though for what purpose is unclear. Perhaps Laura had returned to the house. He did not see Charles but said he saw Susan sitting in a room with a woman he did not recognize. The identity of that woman was never disclosed; perhaps she was Phyllis's mother or another boarder completely uninvolved in the drama unfolding in the house. Benjamin Wright would never again see Susan Watkins alive.

Charles returned to the Washingtons' place after dark. Mr. Washington, still upset at the scandal that had erupted under his roof, confronted him and demanded the answer to the unavoidable question: "whether the white woman or the dark woman was his wife." Further, Washington said he would call for Mack Morris, a Roanoke policeman, and have him arrested. Dejectedly, Charles pointed to Susan and confessed that "this is my lawfully married wife."

The Wrights were gone, and Susan had nowhere to spend the evening. Later, she called the Washingtons into the parlor and asked if she could spend the night in their house. "We agreed to let her stay all night, as she was a stranger," testified Phyllis. Certainly, there was no question of morality here for the landlords—since the two were in truth married, there was no impropriety for a man to spend the night with his wife. In fact, though they hadn't known it before that troubling day, it would be the first time Watkins had slept under their roof and not been in sin.

By all accounts, Susan and Charles spent the night together in his room, Ida being absent. What transpired between them no one else ever knew or now can say. Of course, it strains the imagination to think that anything amorous occurred between the estranged couple. But neither did the Washingtons report overhearing the sound of any arguments. It would be equally hard to imagine them spending a congenial evening catching up. Perhaps they quarreled in strained whispers, hurling insults and accusations pent up by months of separation. It's conceivable that they dozed fitfully, maybe she on the bed, he sitting up in a chair.

Regardless of the unknowable circumstances, it seems to have been a fateful night. Perhaps Charles had spent months conspiring to lure his wife to Virginia with false promises in order to end her inconvenient claim on his life. Or perhaps he never imagined such a thing and was shocked when she appeared at his door that morning.

But it seems likely that, during that tension-filled night spent with the woman he had abandoned, he made his malevolent decision: that Susan Wilson Watkins had to die.

4

"A Fiendish Murder"

Fannie Coxe thought she heard a whippoorwill. She settled down into the cane chair in front of her small cabin and strained her ears. The creek was up, and the cascading water drowned out the usual sounds of the woods around her. Plus her aging ears were not what they once had been. Since she was a girl she'd loved the plaintive cry of a whippoorwill. Of course, there were those who said the bird's call foreshadowed a death. Fannie didn't believe in such nonsense, though. Whippoorwills cried every night, and people somewhere died every night.

She turned her attention back to her sewing, her only source of income. Her sister Mary was a seamstress too, but she had been sick lately, leaving Fannie to do the bulk of the work. Although twilight was deepening and an intermittent rain was falling, there was more light here than indoors and still enough sun to fix this hem.

Some motion caught her eye, and she glanced up to see a woman wading in the rushing stream, avoiding the fallen tree usually used to traverse the creek. Though she wore a veil, Fannie recognized her as Ida, the German girl. Strange woman, thought Fannie, with her Dutchie accent and her predilection for staying with the colored folk. Of course, they say she'd married into the Watkins family up the mountain, which was not the way things worked here in Virginia. She'd even stayed up there at the Watkins house a few months back when she was sick, but Fannie hadn't seen her in a while. Ida passed on, without a greeting or even looking over at the cabin of the two spinster sisters.

Fannie turned back to her sewing, racing the growing gloom of evening. More than an hour passed. She'd have to quit soon—it was nearly too dark to thread the next needle. She lit a small lamp, but oil cost money and she didn't want to burn it long. Better to finish up and go to bed. She decided to stitch until she heard their old clock, one of the few extravagances the sisters had, strike nine.

The clock was still silent when she heard another sound, this one strange—a sort of doleful crying rising over the babble of the creek. Someone else was at the log bridge. Straining her eyes, she could make out two shadowy figures on opposite ends of the fallen tree. "Come on across the log, woman!" she heard an angry male voice say.

"I can't see to walk that log!" replied a woman, her voice strained. Who in the world was out there this time of night?

"I'll get a lantern. You stay there." She saw the man start toward the cabin.

"Who's there?" demanded Fannie, standing up.

"It's me, Charlie Watkins, Miss Coxe. I came up on the dummy to see grandma. Can I borrow a lantern? I'm out here with my wife, and she can't see to cross the log."

Fannie said nothing in return, but she was confused. His wife? Wasn't Ida his wife? She'd crossed the creek thirty minutes ago. Who was the lady weeping on the other bank?

Mary had heard the commotion too and, wrapped in a quilt, came out with a lamp, struck a match and lit it. Together they met Charles and handed him the lantern, then followed him over to the log, if nothing else to see who this stranger woman was. Fannie heard the clock begin chiming its nine times.

Carrying the lamp, Charles crossed the log and coaxed the woman to follow him, holding her arm. Fannie didn't recognize her. She was colored and surprisingly well dressed to be trying to cross a fallen tree over a swollen creek in a rainy forest at night.

Charles turned to the sisters once they were across. "Thank you, Miss Fannie, Miss Mary. Much obliged." He gave no indication of returning the lamp. The woman looked at the sisters fleetingly but said nothing. Fannie could tell she was still upset. Was there fear in her eyes? A silent imploring for help? What was happening here?

However, the couple continued up the path toward Charles's grandmother's house with no further explanation. The Coxe sisters watched them go, surrounded by a circle of weak lamplight. "You see that we get our lantern back!" called Fannie after them. Charlie shouted back, "I'll see that Taylor brings your lamp in the morning."

As they turned back to their cabin in the darkness, Fannie thought she heard the whippoorwill again. She shivered and, taking one last look at the darkened landscape, picked up her small lamp and ducked into the cabin.

The next day of Susan Watkins's life—the last day of Susan Watkins's life—is considerably murkier in the historical record. Nothing in the scanty records indicates how she spent the bulk of the hours of April 6, 1891. Where and what did she eat? Was Charles civil to her in conversation or discourteous and accusatory? Did she give her wayward husband a much-deserved piece of her mind? What plans did she have for the next day? She never returned to the depot to pick up her trunks—did she envision that rather than staying in Virginia she would, after all, leave in a day or two?

On Monday morning, it seems that Charles left early, probably to go to work. Both George and Phyllis Washington testified that he had departed their boardinghouse before they awoke. It is less clear where Susan was that morning—no testimony or press coverage clearly addresses the question. However, it seems likely that she spent the day at the Washingtons' boardinghouse.

Interestingly, the *Roanoke Times* would report that during the afternoon Susan had confided to Phyllis that she was afraid to go anywhere with her husband. Assuming this to be an accurate report and that Phyllis was the source, it raises interesting questions. It's possible that the paper was referring to the similar conversation the two women had the day before; however, it could be that Susan twice expressed apprehension about being alone with Charles. Whatever her frame of mind, it did not ultimately prevent her from going with her husband.

Charles returned about 5:00 p.m. and soon after departed with Susan. Phyllis recalled that she last saw them walking toward downtown Roanoke. How did Charles convince Susan to accompany him? Did he tell her where they were going? Did she go entirely willingly, or did she feel compelled? We can know no answers to these questions.

One possibility suggests itself. Charles had allegedly written to Susan months earlier that he had inherited his grandfather's farm, supposedly as bait to lure her to Virginia and to her doom. Perhaps he enticed her out of the city to see this property at Gum Spring. Did she still have illusions that she and her chastised husband would happily share a life together, farming on the mountainside?

The next recorded sighting of the couple came from a Captain J.C. Hathaway, the conductor on the dummy (streetcar) that ran between Roanoke and Salem. He testified that he saw Charles board his car with a "colored woman," recalling her as articulate and quite well dressed. Hathaway, testifying months later, mistakenly said the day was Sunday instead of Monday, and he could not recall if they bought tickets for the 5:30 or 7:00 run. The former seems most likely, as they were next seen in Salem about 7:00 p.m. and the trip between the two cities was about forty minutes.

Another passenger, T.J. Wilson, also saw them on the dummy, and described Susan as "gingerbread" in complexion. Both he and Hathaway mentioned Susan's unexpectedly elegant attire and especially noted her sealskin coat.

About 7:00 p.m., the Watkins were seen on Main Street in Salem, where they got off the streetcar when it reached its terminus. A passerby, Isaiah Reynolds, recognized Charles outside of Younger's, a Main Street drugstore operated by the mayor of Salem. He was with a woman Reynolds did not recognize and was smoking a cigar.

From there, the couple began a walk of about two miles west along Main Street, through the downtown area, past Lake Spring Hotel, where Charles had worked the previous summer, and past the large new tannery that had sprung up late in Salem's boom years. No witnesses came forward to describe their long walk up Main Street, but it couldn't have been an easy one. Susan certainly would have been used to walking places. She was born into an age when walking was an unavoidable necessity; but she had also been a city-dweller most of her adult life, and this may have been a strenuous trek for her. While Main Street was macadamized and so an easier path than any parallel muddy track, the weather was rainy, even blowing snow. Susan wore shoes that—like a lot of women's footwear through the ages—were crafted more for looks than comfortable endurance.

According to witness testimony, it took them some two hours to go two miles across mostly flat ground—a rate of speed that would suggest frequent stopping along the way. Were they arguing? Was Susan exhausted after two stressful days and a likely sleepless night? Was she reluctant to proceed? Why didn't she turn back or seek refuge at Ben Wright's house nearby? Was Charles impatient to get to his destination before dark?

Or was he timing their approach precisely so they would be in an isolated place after darkness?

The next time anyone recalled encountering the couple was about 9:00 p.m. Charles and Susan had finally veered off the paved road and turned north toward Gum Spring. This road would have been little more than a rutted dirt path running parallel to a creek today called Horner's Branch.

It's unclear how far the couple followed the dirt road before they seemed to join an even more rugged footpath. It was a more direct route to their destination—Charles's grandmother's house—but involved crossing the creek at least once. It was now dark; the branch was swollen with recent rains. The next night would be the new moon, so even the heavens were dark. Charles had grown up on this mountain; he was presumably accustomed to the route, and it presented no challenges to him, even after sunset. But for Susan, this dark, wet, uneven, unfamiliar track was a final straw, especially when they came to the only bridge across the creek: a fallen log.

It's not hard to imagine the scene: Charles, the former farmhand who had crossed this creek and this log hundreds of times, urging Susan, the well-dressed urbanite in fancy shoes, to traverse the wet, slippery tree, nearly

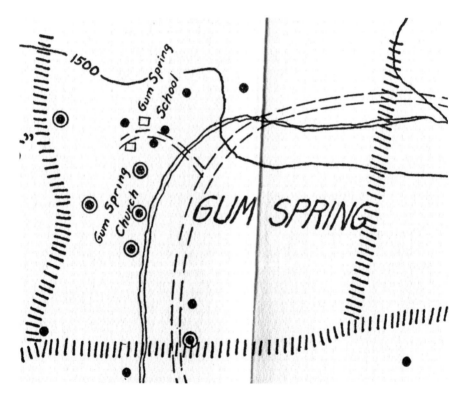

This map, from a 1930 community study of west Roanoke County, is the earliest one to show the Gum Spring neighborhood. The Watkins cabin was in sight of the school. *From "Fort Lewis: A Community in Transition," Institute for Research in the Social Sciences, University of Virginia, 1930.*

invisible in the darkness, as easily as he did. She balked. To her, a bridge was a flat, wide, well-engineered structure with rails, not a piece of fallen timber. She was desperate and terrified; his words grew heated. He impatiently tried to force her across the log; she steadfastly refused. Finally, he agreed to fetch a lantern and return, so at least she'd be able to see.

The log was in sight of the cabin of two sisters, Sarah Frances "Fannie" and Mary Coxe.[15] Charles would have known them for years; he felt perfectly comfortable approaching their home and asking to borrow a lantern. According to Fannie's testimony, he told them that his wife needed light to cross the log; but this could have only confused her—as far as she knew, Ida Friebel was the wife of Charles Watkins. Nevertheless, the sisters loaned him a lamp and sent the couple on the way.

Fannie recalled the approximate time that Charles and Susan passed by—it was within minutes of her clock striking nine.

Between ten and eleven o'clock, Mat Bailey, a resident of the neighborhood, heard shots ring through the dripping woods—four volleys, he recalled. Lucy Watkins would report that she also heard shots, though she recalled only two.

Sometime after that, about 11:00 p.m., Charles Watkins arrived at his grandmother's cabin, distraught and disheveled. And alone.

Friebel was already there when Charles arrived. The historical record tells us little of her whereabouts and actions of the previous twenty-four hours. Almost certainly at some point she must have conferred with Charles, arranging to meet him at the Watkins cabin in Gum Spring. If she was part of a conspiracy to do harm to Susan Watkins, it's unclear what her role was to be.

Ida most likely took the streetcar from Roanoke to Salem an hour or two before Charles and Susan followed her. While in Salem, she took the opportunity to stop at the home of Ben and Mary Wright. She told Mary (it's unclear if Ben was at home) that she was going to "Grandma's" up the mountain and asked to borrow a navy-blue veil, promising to return it in the morning. "Well," she said to Mary, "ain't we in a mess?" She assured Mary that she had a marriage certificate at home in Wisconsin that would prove Susan's claim invalid and said she had sent for it. "You'll see who is right!" she proclaimed. Mary's reactions were not recorded.

From there, Ida headed west, passing the Coxe cabin about 7:00 p.m., and arriving at the Watkins cabin at 7:35 p.m. Maria Watkins, Charles's grandmother, was presumably there, as was her son Taylor and his wife,

Lucy. No one expected Ida, but she had not been out of their thoughts that day. Word had reached the cabin in the afternoon, traveling at the speed of small-town gossip, of the appearance of another claimant to the name Mrs. Charles Watkins.

Ida's clothes were wet, and she explained that she'd waded the creek and come through the wet field below. Lucy invited her to take off her wet shoes and warm up. To Lucy, Ida looked worried and like she'd "been crying herself to death." Understandably, Lucy "didn't know how to receive her." What does one say in such a circumstance?

Yet snippets of their conversation survive. Ida said that Charles would be coming behind her. She gave some account of Susan's arrival in town and reiterated her claim that she and Charles were legitimately married. The talk turned to brutally practical matters: sometime before, Ida had borrowed money from Taylor and Lucy, and she promised to repay that debt soon. She had wired her family in Wisconsin for money and expected it imminently. Indeed, within the next few days she would cash a fifty-dollar check from her father, Henry Friebel of Dodge County, Wisconsin, but it is unclear when (or why) she had telegraphed the request. It certainly could indicate an intention to leave town in a hurry.

It was "right smart in the night" when Charles arrived at the cabin, his uncle Taylor reported.

Charles, seemingly an emotional wreck, spoke with his uncle, who tried to ascertain what was happening. The visitor said by way of explanation that he had come to see his ill grandmother (who must have been in the house but remained in bed the entire time). But inevitably, the conversation turned to Susan's arrival in town. Charles conceded that a woman had arrived in Roanoke the day before, claiming to be his true wife. He also claimed that she had threatened him and Ida with bodily harm.

Charles had not been at the house long when he peered out the door into the darkness. Suddenly, he called to Taylor, "Someone is coming by the schoolhouse!" Taylor walked out on the porch and saw a woman approaching through the darkness, "like Banquo's ghost," a prosecutor would later dramatically claim. "Who's that, who's that?" he called. But he knew soon enough as she approached. It was Susan.

Frightened, Lucy and Ida retreated into a back room, afraid a confrontation would ensue. They remained out of sight, and Lucy would claim she never laid eyes on Susan.

The mysterious woman ignored Taylor and pushed past him through the open door. She was wet, muddy and bleeding from a wound to her neck. She held her left arm, and a bloody handkerchief was wrapped around her left hand. She was in pain and clearly in need of assistance. And yet compassion was not to be found at the Watkins cabin.

"Why did you shoot me?" Susan demanded of Charles.

"Who says I shot you?" he responded—a rather ridiculous rejoinder on its face. "You know you did," she challenged. "I want you to have this ball taken out of my hand. I want a doctor."

It was an understandable demand. Although Susan was also bleeding from a wound to her neck, it was more superficial, and the bullet lodged in her hand or wrist apparently caused her more pain. After being attacked, she must have arisen, in shock, in pain and struggled on through the moonless, rainy woods. She couldn't know where she was going; she couldn't find her way back to the Coxe cabin below, much less to town, without aid. She was certainly in no shape to cross the treacherous log bridge again. But perhaps she could see a light at the Watkins cabin and hear voices—the only things she could see and hear.

To anyone else, she would have been a subject of sympathy. The nearest doctor was probably in Salem, three miles or so away. It would take hours to send for one, hours for him to return. Still, the sudden visitor needed medical care, and the compassionate thing to do would be to send immediately for a physician. Young Lawrence Anderson[16] couldn't have been far away; neighbors Mat Bailey and John Banks lived together in the vicinity. Any of these could have been awakened and dispatched for help.

And yet, no one was willing to meet the desperate request of a wounded woman.

Charles flat-out refused to go—he likely understood that such an errand of mercy would result in his arrest. Susan then turned to Taylor and asked for his help. Taylor's answer is more inexplicable. He said he could not take her to a doctor or fetch her any medical assistance—because he had to arise early the next morning to go to work at the Pierpont Brickyard.

How could Taylor, by all accounts a responsible and respected citizen of the neighborhood, so callously refuse a request for help from a person in dire and obvious need? There is no easy answer, but perhaps familial ties played a role. Charles, flaws and all, was family, as in a sense was Ida, hiding in the room beyond. This woman, whom none of them had ever seen until a few minutes ago, was an outsider, pitiable though she may have been. And she was, in a sense, a menace, potentially a dangerous one. Did she mean them harm?

The Pierpont Brick Yard in West Roanoke County, where Taylor Watkins was employed. *Rich Huggins.*

It might now seem ridiculous to think of the slight, well-dressed, bedraggled and bleeding woman as a threat to the occupants of the cabin. However, it may be that the family looked at her just in that way. Months later, and weeks after the trial had concluded, the *Roanoke Times* reported that Charles had given authorities a confession. As we shall see, there is reason to take this admission of guilt with a grain of salt—the *Times* had reason to maximize sales by sensationalizing the Watkins affair. But one detail—if reported accurately—may help us reconstruct the mindset of Taylor and Lucy Watkins. In the "confession," Charles allegedly told his uncle and aunt upon arrival at the cabin that he had "shot that damned western wife of mine down yonder just now, and I think I killed her, goddamn her." He then added that he had acted only after *she* had threatened *him*. He had done it in self-defense.

A ludicrous assertion, no doubt, and contrary to facts that would come out later, but if Taylor and Lucy believed it (bearing in mind that no one had had time to think things through at that point), when Susan arrived they may have not seen a wounded woman who needed help. They may have seen an adversary. This is not to defend their refusal to help an injured person but to find an explanation for it.

Perhaps the Watkins clan was instinctively protecting the honor of the family. It's worth noting that, while virtually all of Charles's relatives with knowledge of the case would eventually testify against him in court, they never seemed to have said all they could.

There is evidence of the family protecting Charles. Within a couple of days, Lucy Watkins would demonstrably misrepresent the events of the night while under oath. At the coroner's inquest later in the week, Lucy would fail to mention the fact—the extremely relevant fact—that an injured Susan came to the house that night. In fact, that detail seemed to have remained hidden for months. Only much later when called on this omission in the courtroom, Lucy would say (accurately) that she only answered questions she was directly asked, and no one asked her if Susan had been to her home. She did testify that she had never seen Susan, which may have been technically true since she remained concealed in a back room with Ida that night.

None of this suggests the mindset of a witness eager to help investigators come to the truth of the matter. The rest of the night of April 6–7 could only have been a strained, uncomfortable affair. Denied medical assistance, Susan attempted to explain herself, perhaps win an ally. She told Taylor that she was Charles's lawful wife and could prove it with the papers she had in her trunks in Roanoke. Taylor's later testimony of that night gives no indication of whether he believed Susan at that time or not.

He asked Susan to sit down; she replied that she preferred not to but asked that Charles be searched. Taylor agreed to search his nephew's pockets; he found only a medicine vial, otherwise undescribed. It is evident that Charles had a gun, but what became of it was seemingly never discovered. Later, in a self-serving account of his activities in April, Charles would mention that he sold his pistol for cash while a fugitive. Perhaps he had hidden the weapon outside and retrieved it later.

Charles, for his part, claimed that he felt threatened by the wounded woman and asked to borrow Taylor's own pistol. His uncle wisely declined.

Charles and Susan began to argue—"have some words," Taylor gently called it. But it didn't last long. Susan abruptly ended the confrontation by announcing that she had no intention of fighting. All she wanted was for her husband "to have the ball taken out of her hand, give her money to go back home, and [Charles] could have the white wench."

There is no detail given of the rest of the night, except that everyone in the cabin remained awake and relatively calm—there was no further "fussy

Dillard's Drugstore, Main Street, Salem. "Doc" Watts Dillard is second from the right, leaning against the doorpost. *Salem Historical Society*.

talk," in the words of Lucy Watkins. She and Ida remained concealed in the back room, and presumably, Susan was unaware of their presence. At some point, Charles entered the back room to talk with Ida. The two lay across a bed and conversed in whispers. There can be only speculation about the tenor of that conversation.

At dawn, around 6:00 a.m., Charles departed with Susan, ostensibly to take her to "Doc Dillard's" in Salem to have her hand treated and the bullet extracted. Watts Dillard was actually a pharmacist, not a physician, although small towns in the nineteenth century often drew no distinction between the two.

When the couple left the Watkins cabin, it was the last confirmed time anyone would see Susan alive.[17]

About three hours later, Charles returned to his grandmother's cabin— alone. Taylor had left for work by then, but Lucy was home. She sensed something was wrong, terribly wrong, and later said she was "too scared" to eat breakfast. Charles gave no explanation (at least none that was recorded) for Susan's absence. He had a cup of coffee and then lay down to rest. A few hours later, about two or three o'clock in the afternoon, he and Ida departed together, headed down the mountain to return to Roanoke.

Not long after that, Lawrence Anderson discovered a body in the creek.

5

"NOW A FUGITIVE FROM JUSTICE"

I t was either tired eyes or a tired brain, but the figures just didn't add up. The error was only a few cents, and it wouldn't be the end of the world if he ignored it or forced it to balance by adding a few cents to an invoice. But that would be admitting defeat, letting the ledger get the better of him. No, best to go over the columns again…

John M. Oakey was hunched over his roll-top desk and getting a headache from staring at the neatly printed numbers. Running two undertaking establishments meant more profit but also more accounting. Things were easier when he had just the Salem shop, and selling furniture was the main focus of the business. But a good furniture craftsman could also make a good coffin, and there was an endless demand for that line of merchandise.

Opening up the second location in Roanoke was good business, he knew. He'd been one of the first to recognize that the little village of Big Lick was going to grow into a big railroad center in short order. A boomtown needs undertakers just like it needs grocers and dentists and farriers. Good business, but a more complicated life and more confounding bookkeeping. Not to mention the travel time. When his duties required a trip to Roanoke, the streetcar ride from Salem was about forty minute each way, almost an hour and a half gone from his busy days. Oakey had adopted the habit of whiling away the time on the dummy with the hobby that relaxed his mind, a beloved, if unusual, pastime. Of course, some folks looked at him oddly, a prominent man of trade in dark business attire, clacking together knitting needles on the streetcar. But let them stare, he thought.

JOHN MARTIN OAKEY

Undertaker John M. Oakey. *Salem Historical Society.*

Oakey heard the door open and close, and he half stood up to see if it was a customer entering. Instead, he recognized the boy who delivered telegrams. "Western Union for you, Mr. Oakey!" the lad called. "Well, I imagine that's my invitation from President Harrison to come up to the White House for dinner," responded Oakey, as he always did. And as he always did, the boy responded with a wide smile at the joke. Oakey took the envelope, tousled the boy's hair and flipped a nickel tip at him. With a thank-you, the boy ran back out on Main Street.

Oakey sat back down at his desk and opened the envelope. He read the short notice and sighed deeply. "I do not know a Susan Watkins and will not be responsible for any debts incurred," read the message.

Suddenly, he felt very tired. He put down the telegram and rubbed his eyes beneath his spectacles. Well, the message was clear, but he didn't understand it. Had he contacted the wrong man in Chicago? He was pretty sure, from the little bit anyone knew about the poor murdered woman lying in a new pine coffin across the room, that he'd sent the telegraph to the right person. But if he denied being her brother, there wasn't much to do about it.

It was this sort of thing that bothered Oakey the most about his business. Here was a lady who'd come all the way across the country to find her husband, only to be betrayed by him in the worst possible manner. Now she'd been abandoned by her family as well. He knew next to nothing about Mrs. Watkins—no one in town did. But she deserved better than this.

Well, at least she'll get a decent burial. Standing up, Oakey walked out back of the building to talk to old Dick, his faithful gravedigger. Dick Gholston had worked for Oakey for years and dug hundreds of graves up on East Hill. He found the old man in the shed in the back, repairing a harness for the hearse.

"Richard, it looks like we'll have to bury Mrs. Watkins here. Think you can find her a place in your people's cemetery?" It meant a pauper's grave, paid for by the county, but he knew the black community of Salem would handle the service with dignity and solemnity, just as if she'd grown up here in Salem.

Gholston stood up and rubbed his chin. "Yessir. The ground's heavy after all this rain, but I expect I can get it done this afternoon. Want me to ask Pastor Fox to read the services?"

"Yes, if you would. Ugly business, this Watkins case."

"Yessir. Ugly business. But Pastor Fox'll do right by her." Gholston got his pick and shovel and started to walk to the colored cemetery just out of town.

Oakey watched him go for a few minutes. Seeing Gholston with his tools slung over his shoulder reminded Oakey of a decision he'd already made: when the time came—and it could be soon—for someone else to dig Old Dick's grave, Oakey would put it next to his own family's plot. Of course, black men weren't buried in the white cemetery as a matter of course, but Oakey would see to it. He would also put a pick and shovel on the gravestone so people for generations would recognize his significance. Richard deserved a dignified memorial.

Of course, so did Mrs. Watkins, Oakey thought again. He turned to go back to his stubborn columns of figures.[18]

THE MURDER OF SUSAN Watkins threw the quiet community of Salem and west Roanoke County into a frenzy—part outrage, part sympathy, part voyeurism. It was a clear tragedy, but also a novel event. While murders were not unheard of in the Roanoke Valley, they were more likely to occur in the boisterous city of Roanoke than the quiet rural areas. In fact, the *Roanoke Times* broke the story of the Watkins murder on Thursday, April 9, under the headline "High Carnival of Crime." Susan's homicide coincided with the murder of a Nat Newson, an African American drayman in Roanoke. (The crime occurred, in fact, on Sixth Avenue NE, the same street as the Washingtons' boardinghouse). A third murder, of a night watchman in nearby Bluefield, West Virginia, rounded out the "High Carnival" reported in that morning's papers. The alleged perpetrator of the Bluefield crime, one Alexander Foote, was lynched by a mob of fifty men a few days later.

The *Salem Times-Register*, a weekly published on Friday, reported the Watkins story a day later, under the headline "A Fiendish Murder."

Almost as soon as Lawrence Anderson reported the discovery of Susan's body, she became a spectacle. People in the Gum Spring neighborhood flocked to the isolated stretch of Horner's Branch to gaze on her and exchange shocked whispers. Neighbors, no doubt gathering details of the night before from the Watkins family and the Coxe sisters, quickly and uniformly placed guilt for the crime on Charles Watkins.

The news of the murder did not reach Salem, and therefore the authorities, until almost sundown, too late to begin an investigation. To keep the crime scene secure until an investigation could be organized, two men from the vicinity, John Banks and Samuel Strickler, both African American, were appointed to stand guard over the body all of Tuesday night, presumably by county sheriff Charles M. Webber.

When discovered, the remains of Susan Wilson Watkins were lying in the creek but on a "little drift" partially out of the stream. Her head was in the water, her skirt partially up around her waist. Her pockets were turned out as if they'd been searched; however, her jewelry was undisturbed. Furthermore, one stocking was pulled down and the garter missing. This led the *Roanoke Times* to speculate that her pocketbook and the money it contained may have been held in the garter. Ben Wright had seen her wallet and a considerable amount of cash at his house, but it was not found on the body, presumably removed by the killer or an accomplice.

Early on Wednesday, the eighth, an official coroner's inquest convened at the crime scene, which the press ominously called Dark Hollow. A coroner's inquest (or coroner's jury) in nineteenth-century Virginia would be charged with investigating any death of a suspicious nature and served a variety of functions carried out today by more professionalized elements of law enforcement. The inquest was empowered to determine a cause of death, interrogate witnesses, consider evidence and ultimately recommend charges. In this particular case, the jury was charged "upon the view of the body of Susie Watkins, there lying dead…to enquire when, how, and by what means the said Susie Watkins came to her death."[19]

Members of the jury included J. Ed Shipman, Lewis Coffman, Charles Hatcher and Frank Lovelock. Lovelock was a reporter for the *Roanoke Times* and undoubtedly the source of the information that was printed the next day. In addition, Banks and Strickler, the African American guards from the previous night, were appointed jurors, making the panel an interracial one. Dr. B.P. Saunders and Dr. T.M. Baird provided the jury with medical expertise.

Heading up the inquest was John H. Camper, a local justice of the peace serving at the time as acting coroner for Roanoke County. He and members of the jury examined the site, taking careful note of such details as whether the body's resting place could be seen from the adjacent path (not easily), identifiable footprints and the gold watch found on the body. Charles Hatcher observed carefully enough that he would be able to identify the watch in court months later.

When the jury was satisfied with its investigation of the crime scene, Susan's remains were taken to the undertaking establishment of John M. Oakey in Salem. "All day long throngs of colored men and women visited Oakey's establishment to see the dead woman," reported the *Roanoke Times*.

Per the usual procedure, the next order of business was to have a physician conduct an inspection of the remains. Dr. Saunders, assisted by Baird, carried out the postmortem.[20] He found "four wounds of the scalp that seem to have been made by a blunt instrument, such as a rock or club. Two of these wounds were on the back of the head, one from the top, and one behind the left ear. There was hemorrhage of the brain at the points wounded. There was also a fracture of the skull behind the left ear." Dr. Saunders noted the neck wound from the first attempt on her life but dismissed it as a minor puncture wound, perhaps caused when she fell on a branch or twig. He also described "a flesh wound on the left arm." Interestingly, he did not describe either of these latter two injuries as gunshot wounds.

Once this postmortem examination was concluded, there remained the necessity of giving Susan Wilson Watkins a decent burial. Oakey learned, no doubt from the Wrights, that Susan had a brother in Chicago, presumably the one who worked as a guard at a museum. Oakey sent a telegram to the

Modern view of East Hill Cemetery North, Salem's primary burial ground for African Americans (and resting place of Susan Watkins). *Salem Historical Society.*

brother (never named in press accounts) but received only a reply that he "did not know such a person as Susie Watkins." The *Salem Times-Register* conjectured, rather insultingly, that he was "probably thinking that some expense might be connected with the matter."

Why did the brother decline knowing Susan? We can only guess. Perhaps he did wish to avoid the expense of a funeral. Or it is possible the siblings were estranged, and although Charles and Susan had spent some time in Chicago, the brother was unaware of her married name.

Oakey embalmed Susan's remains and arranged her burial at the nearby "colored cemetery" now known as East Hill Cemetery North. She was buried there on Sunday, April 12, 1891. No description of the services survives, but no doubt a local African American pastor was asked to officiate, and a crowd of curious onlookers filled in for mourners. It is likely that the Wrights attended; despite having met her only a week before, they were closest thing Susan Wilson Watkins had to friends in Virginia. Perhaps the Washingtons were there as well, possibly Taylor and Lucy Watkins or other residents of Gum Spring.

The costs of burying a pauper—and in this case Susan qualified—were routinely paid by the Roanoke County Board of Supervisors. However, there is no evidence in their minutes of Oakey submitting the expenses for reimbursement. It is possible he bore the costs himself.

A burial in a pauper's grave, attended only by strangers, and soon forgotten—it only adds to the pathos of Susan Watkins's tragic end.

THE NEXT ORDER OF business for the coroner's inquest was to depose witnesses. People from Roanoke, Salem and the Gum Spring area were summoned to testify—and, per procedure, paid $0.50 each for their trouble. (Jurors received $1.00 each, with Banks and Strickler receiving an additional $1.50 for standing guard. Banks, who also testified as a witness, received a grand total of $3.00.)

Each witness had a piece of the overall story to tell, some big pieces and some small. The job of the inquest was to assemble them, bit by bit, like a quilter joined patchwork into a finished quilt.

Ben and Mary Wright, Phyllis and George Washington, Fannie Coxe and Lawrence Anderson were all deposed and revealed their parts in the drama. The Wrights and the Washingtons, who had spent more time with Susan than anyone else save Charles, certainly were crucial in establishing the identity of the body in the creek. Lucy Watkins testified, but she did not tell all she could. Months later, as noted earlier, Lucy confessed that she withheld information about Susan's visit to their cabin. Indeed, the inquest remained ignorant of the relevant facts that Charles had attacked his wife prior to the actual murder and that Susan had confronted her husband at the Watkins cabin.

Lucy's reticence did not begin with her testimony. On the afternoon Susan's body was found, Addie Anderson, a cousin of Charles's and likely a niece of Taylor, asked Lucy if Charles had brought "the woman" to the cabin the night before. Her answer was telling: "No. God in Heaven knows he did not bring her with him."

Technically, this was true: Susan had arrived separate from Charles and after being injured by him. Why Lucy felt the need to conceal this fact from Addie is not clear, but perhaps she was instinctively defending her kinsman. As demonstrated by the Peter Martin murder some thirteen years before, the African American population of Roanoke County seemed to have an instinctive distrust of a legal system in which they were second-class citizens. Lucy was perhaps hesitant to say much about the case if it could implicate Charles, even though she seemed to have little doubt about his guilt.

Several other witnesses described passing encounters with Charles Watkins: Hathaway, the streetcar conductor; Reynolds, who passed Charles and Susan on the street in Salem; and some who saw Charles and Ida together after the murder. Two men were called whose testimony proved immaterial to the case and was stricken—they had both seen Watkins in Salem, but weeks before the crime. Their testimony was stopped midsentence and literally scratched out of the inquest's minutes.

It is interesting to note who was not on the inquest's witness list. Laura, the daughter of Ben Wright who seems to have spent some time with Ida on Sunday, was not deposed—nor was Mary Coxe or Maria Watkins (though she is at one time quoted in the *Roanoke Times*). Most notably absent was Taylor Watkins. The jury desired to hear from both of the Wrights and both of the Washingtons, but not Taylor alongside his wife. Why? Perhaps the easiest answer is best: he was working and unavailable. Though of course the jury was unaware of the fact, he had more interaction with the suspect and the victim on the night of the murder than anyone. Had his voice been heard, assuming he didn't conceal evidence as his wife did, a large piece of the patchwork could have been added.

While the witnesses were being heard, a deputy named Walter Boon was dispatched to the passenger depot in Roanoke to fetch Susan's trunks, of which the jury no doubt had been informed by Ben Wright. Upon arrival in

Salem town sergeant Jacob B. Frier (*right*) and his deputy Walter Boon (*left*). *Salem Historical Society.*

Salem, the contents of the trunk were examined, including the conclusive evidence that Susan and Charles were in fact legally wed.

By afternoon on April 9, the jury was ready to render its verdict. The panel had heard enough to reach its conclusion—in reality the only conclusion the facts would support: "We the jurors believe that said Susie Watkins came to her death…from wounds on top of the head and fracture of the skull inflicted by a rock, stick, or some other hard instrument in the hands of Charles Watkins." Furthermore, the inquest concluded that "Ida Freibel [*sic*] alias Edith Freibel alias Ida Watkins was an accessory to the act either before or after the fact."

Charles Watkins had become a wanted man and a fugitive from justice. Ida, for her part, had no opportunity to flee the suspicions of authorities. She was already in custody before the inquest named her an accessory.

WHERE DID THE COUPLE go after leaving the cabin in Gum Spring? Once again, witness testimony gives some clues, but a complete picture of the hours after the murder is elusive. About breakfast time, Charles had returned to his grandmother's cabin in Gum Spring and gone to bed. After

Charles awakened, he and Ida secluded themselves in Lucy Watkins's room, seemingly to discuss matters. Lucy reported that "it seemed like he was bothered," adding that he "answered questions." However, Lucy did not elaborate on (or the inquest did not record) what questions were asked or what his answers were. The couple departed the cabin about 2:00 p.m., not long before Susan's body was found in the creek.

Sometime about 3:00 p.m., a nearby resident, William Sims, passed Charles and Ida on the lane adjacent to Fannie Coxe's home. They were next seen by John Banks, the member of the coroner's jury, on the macadamized road, near the Preston Place where Charles had lived for a while as a boy, between 3:00 and 4:00 p.m. By 4:30, they were in downtown Salem, where a W.E. Bower noted them on Main Street and saw them get onto the streetcar, speaking to Mr. Coleman the conductor.

The dummy took them back to Roanoke, where at some point Charles stopped at the Hotel Felix and collected the wages that were due him. In the evening, he returned to the Washingtons' boardinghouse to retrieve his trunk. Phyllis Washington demanded—and received—a full month's rent from Charles, although he and Ida had lived there only half that time. George pointedly asked Charles about Susan, and he responded that he had left her "over on Jefferson Street" in downtown. Before he left the Washingtons for the last time, on a horse-drawn omnibus, Charles dejectedly said to George, "I guess you think hard of me." George conceded that he did indeed. At this point, news of Susan's murder had apparently not yet reached Roanoke, or George's opinion may have been even harder toward his former tenant.

Later on Tuesday night, Charles stopped at the store of a merchant on Salem Avenue, Ed Oppenheimer, and purchased a pint of whiskey. Oppenheimer reported that Charles was surprisingly conversational, giving him much of his background before departing. It is unclear where Charles and Ida spent the night of April 7–8.

The next morning, Ida went to a bank and cashed a check for fifty dollars sent from her father, Henry, in Wisconsin, a check she had told Lucy Watkins was on the way. Exactly when she received the check, or when or why she requested it from her parents, is unclear. Afterward, she arrived at the Washington home to collect her possessions. Apparently, because the ongoing coroner's inquest wanted to question both Charles Watkins and Ida Friebel, when she arrived at the boardinghouse she was promptly arrested by waiting authorities. The *Salem Times-Register* indicated there was some other charge outstanding against her, but if that was accurate, no detail was given.

WHERE WAS CHARLES? WHY did the couple split up? Why did they go to the boardinghouse to claim their trunks separately? Was it all Charles's self-serving plan—removing himself from risk of arrest and abandoning Ida to her fate? For his part, Charles would later claim that he regretted greatly leaving her. He claimed, perhaps self-servingly, that an unnamed friend in Roanoke tipped him off that Ida had been arrested and admonished him to "go as fast as cars can carry you," adding that if Charles escaped "they can't do anything with her." This assessment ultimately proved to be accurate—absent the main suspect, no charge could be made against Edith Friebel.

The account of Charles's movements is murky at best and was clouded even more by rumor, misapprehensions and mistaken identities. Under questioning soon after her arrest, Ida indicated that she did not know Charles's whereabouts but that they were to meet in the nearby town of Liberty (modern Bedford, Virginia). Whether this was true is another matter.

Ida's statement had an effect: it seemed to direct the attention of the authorities to Liberty in Bedford County. By Friday, rumors reached Roanoke and Salem that Charles had been arrested at Liberty and would be returned imminently. It was a false report, and it served to delay the search for the fugitive by twelve crucial hours. "It is feared he has made good his escape," lamented the *Roanoke Times*. The *Salem Times-Register* speculated that he had not gone far and was in fact hiding out in the mountains surrounding the Roanoke Valley. It's unclear what the source of this rumor was, but it seemed solid enough to dispatch the Jeff Davis Rifles—a local militia unit that would serve in the Spanish-American War in a few years—to spend days combing the mountains.

In fact, Charles had passed through Bedford County, but his destination was Lynchburg, a much larger city farther along the rail lines. He later speciously claimed to have stopped there for a shave at a barbershop, and it was while sitting in the barber's chair that he first heard of the death of Susan. He also claimed to have overheard two African American men, part of the developing manhunt, discussing the prospects of arresting him, completely unaware that the fugitive was sitting there with a towel over his face. Still later he would deny this story and say he found out about Susan's death by reading the Lynchburg paper. Both versions were, of course, the statements of a suspect maintaining that he had nothing to do with his wife's death.

From Lynchburg, Charles proceeded, according to one account he gave later, to Richmond and caught a train on the Richmond and Danville

Railroad for North Carolina, making it all sound like an uneventful and carefree trek. But in another account, a letter to Ben Wright that became a key piece of evidence in his trial, Charles painted a much bleaker account of his journey: He said that he "started a foot walk, two hundred miles, and then I was nearly dead, so I got on the train and rode until all my money was gone, rings, overcoat, pistol and everything else. Ben, I look[ed] like a tramp."

Which of these accounts is most accurate we cannot say, but for the moment it indeed looked as if Charles had "made good his escape." For the moment, he had literally gotten away with murder.

CHARLES HAD EVERY REASON to want to disappear. For obvious reasons, he wanted to evade law enforcement, but there was another, possibly more immediate, threat. From the first mention of his name in the papers, it was reported that Charles would not stand trial if apprehended. Instead, he would be lynched—and by Roanoke County's *African American* population.

Lynchings of suspects in criminal cases were shamefully common in the nineteenth-century South. Usually, the victim was an African American accused of a crime or even of a breach of the strict racial protocols of the day. The accusations were too often false; even if there was some evidence of a crime, seldom, if ever, had any guilt been proven in a court of law. The perpetrators were generally white mobs, sometimes even prominent members of a locality's society. But black-on-black lynchings, while comparatively rare in late nineteenth-century America, were not unknown. One scholar estimated that between 1882 and 1892, there were seventy-eight cases of African Americans lynching a member of their own race, though none in Virginia. There were even four incidents of blacks lynching whites in the South.[21]

Almost as soon as the case hit the papers, lurid—and apparently unsubstantiated—rumors of angry lynch mobs forming were voiced. The *Roanoke Times* reported on April 9 that "some of the Negroes of Salem and the County" had turned out to search the countryside for the suspected murderer and that an unnamed "second cousin" of Charles Watkins had predicted he would be lynched if caught by this posse. The same story further claimed that plans to lynch Ida Friebel were also in the works.

The next day, the *Times* again reported that some African Americans ("bolder than the rest" of those merely curious about the case) "freely indulged in threats to lynch the murderer when caught." But law enforcement officials were on guard against the threat and determined "to protect the accused." When the false rumor that Charles had been apprehended in Bedford reached Salem, "a mob of several hundred Negroes" reportedly began to mill about the jail. When Sheriff Webber announced that Watkins was not in custody, the crowd dispersed.

The *Salem Times-Register*, however, thought the lynch mob rumors to be nothing more than gossip and yellow journalism, enflamed by the daily paper in the larger city next door. On April 17, the writers acknowledged "some excitement" had ensued after the false report of an arrest, but the "street rumors" of lynch mobs in formation were dismissed as so much "bosh."

Ultimately, none of the lynch mob predictions came to fruition—nor could they, since Charles Watkins was nowhere to be found. Still, the brief furor gives an interesting glimpse into the Roanoke Valley of 1891. That the rumors of plans to lynch Watkins persisted indicates the depth of feeling in the African American community concerning the case. Sympathies, not surprisingly, seemed to be entirely with the victim, not the suspect, despite the fact that Charles was a native and Susan a complete stranger.

While of course the threat of a lynch mob was an unlawful reaction to any crime, if true, it would seem to have been motivated by a certain misdirected sense of justice: the murdered woman deserved to be vindicated and the murderer punished in no uncertain terms. As things would transpire, justice would indeed be done—but by the proper legal authorities, not a lynch mob.

WHILE CHARLES WAS A man in the shadows, Ida Friebel was behind bars in the Roanoke County jail in Salem. She had been arrested less than twenty-four hours after the discovery of Susan's body and while the coroner's jury was still deliberating. There could not yet have been any firm evidence linking her to the crime, yet Deputy Sheriff Henry Webber (a brother of Sheriff Charles Webber) moved swiftly to place her under arrest.

As far as we can know, Ida had never been incarcerated in her twenty-three years, and press accounts indicate it was anything but a pleasant experience for her. A certain amount of sympathy comes through from newspaper stories—it fit the favored narrative of the crime that a misguided country girl had been duped by a suave lothario into not just an interracial, adulterous love affair but one that turned homicidal. Watkins is the villain of the story, Susan the innocent victim. But Edith Friebel was painted somewhere in between the two—and initially closer to the victim pole. She was also presented as a negative moral example—don't let this happen to your daughter.

The *Salem Times-Register* claimed the first interview with Ida, no doubt because the publisher, Frank Webber, was yet another brother of the sheriff. The writer found her "weeping and well-nigh crazed with grief," and described her as "not very bright mentally.... [S]he doesn't converse with the sly cunning of a hardened criminal." Further, she "has been a Catholic, but realizes that by her immoral life she has sinned deeply, and if it were possible she would willingly return to her home and try to lead a respectable life, but is afraid that her father may not receive her."

Not unexpectedly, she maintained her innocence and her ignorance of the murder. But melodramatically, the paper proclaimed that "deserted by her kinsfolk, estranged from her church, she knows not what may happen next and in her unhappy, wretched and friendless condition she prays for death." The writer also speculated that "should Charles Watkins be caught there is but little doubt that she will tell all she knows" and opined that it was his "firm conviction…that she had no knowledge of the crime, nor was she an accessory by word or deed."

Staff of the *Salem Times-Register*. Frank Webber stands in the doorway. *Salem Historical Society.*

Charles   Frank   Henry

The three Webber brothers of Salem: Sheriff Charles Webber, newspaperman Frank Webber and Deputy/Detective Henry Webber. *Charlie Webber.*

Meanwhile, the *Roanoke Times* described a letter she wrote to her parents, drawing at the bottom of the page a cross flanked with the words "Father" and "Mother" and the entreaty "Pray for me!"

Ida was held in custody, uncharged, until April 25. By that time, she had hired an attorney, Colonel George W. Hansbrough. Hansbrough's son and law partner, Livingston Hansbrough, was the commonwealth's attorney for Roanoke County; however, no one seemed to find this a conflict of interest, perhaps because the latter's term was coming to an end.

The elder Hansbrough, said the *Salem Times-Register*, "had an easy task to obtain her release, for there was no evidence against her." Indeed, although she had been named an accessory to the murder by the coroner's jury, there was no way to charge her with any crime. If she had conspired with Charles to plan the homicide, the only possible person who could testify of that would be Charles himself, who was missing.

Further, she had an ironclad alibi. Taylor and Lucy Watkins could (and almost certainly did) testify truthfully that she was with them at the time the crime was perpetrated.

And so Edith became a free woman again.

Ida left the jail, indicating to the jailer that she intended to go to Cincinnati, Ohio. She immediately caught the streetcar to Roanoke and first went to the home of Mrs. Sheppard, where she and Charles had lived before moving to the Washingtons' house. Sheppard and Ida seemed to have maintained a close relationship, and it's possible that her house was where Ida had stayed the missing nights after Susan's arrival in Roanoke.

Soon after, the two women left the house to go to the depot nearby. Almost immediately, they were spotted and questioned by an unnamed *Roanoke Times* reporter, who had obviously trailed Edith and who was perhaps the same Lovelock who had served on the coroner's jury. She made no effort to conceal her identity or to avoid answering questions.

Not surprisingly, she maintained her innocence—and that of Charles. She claimed, contrary to the evidence uncovered by the inquest, that Charles was in Roanoke at the time of the murder, offering no proof of the claim nor being challenged by the reporter on it.

Further, Ida told the reporter that she had been unjustly incarcerated for two weeks and that the papers had misrepresented her story. This may well be true. One paper, the *Roanoke Herald*, of which no copies survive, was frequently lambasted by both the *Roanoke Times* and the *Salem Times-Register* for being too sensationalistic at the expense of accuracy. It was the *Herald* reporter (identified only as a Mr. Beckner) who had reported that Charles had been found in Bedford, with the effect of delaying the search for him elsewhere. Later, the *Herald* reported on a letter Edith had written in German to her parents, which the *Times* (with better contacts in the jail) said was a wholesale fraud. In fact, both the *Times* and the *Times-Register* indicated that the *Herald* writer had so antagonized Deputy Webber that he had been denied access to the jail at all. The *Herald*, in modern parlance, seemed to specialize in "fake news."

But then, it's easy for the modern reader to conclude that both of the other papers were also sensationalizing the case.

When asked where she was going, Ida said she planned to return home to Wisconsin, and to get there she said she had twenty-five dollars, the sum remaining after paying Colonel Hansbrough to secure her release. This was presumably from the fifty dollars her father had sent her before her arrest, although months later it would be alleged by Charles that Edith may have obtained money from a much more gruesome source: the body of Susan Watkins.

Presently, the two ladies, reporter in tow, arrived at the depot. The ticket counter was closed at the time, and Ida was heard to say to Mrs. Sheppard, "Let's walk over there now. Maybe we can see him before the train comes." Whom she intended to meet was never made clear; the two women walked toward nearby Salem Avenue, stopped and conferred in whispers, then abandoned their quest and returned to the depot.

By the time the two women arrived back at the station, the ticket windows were open, but a large crowd had formed. An increasingly agitated Edith tried to find an opening to purchase a ticket, with Chicago her preferred destination. Whether this represented a change in her plans or if Chicago was part of the itinerary to Wisconsin is unclear. At any rate, she failed to buy a ticket by the time the next train departed.

This was intolerable for Edith, who was clearly, and understandably, eager to leave Virginia. Whatever great adventure she had envisioned when she moved to the South, it could not have included being implicated in a murder, abandoned by her lover and spending two weeks in jail.

She grew visibly agitated. When she finally got to a ticket counter, she took the next available train, to Harrisburg, Pennsylvania, letting the reporter know she would catch a train to Chicago from there.

She made another intriguing comment to the *Times* reporter before she got on the train. She remarked that "she had been released from jail for a purpose," adding (perhaps not entirely accurately) that she had "made no particular effort to get out." This led her to conclude that the authorities had released her for one reason.

They wanted her to lead detectives to the fugitive Charles Watkins.

But she also told the reporter in no uncertain terms that "she was too sharp for that. They would never find Watkins by watching her."

INDEED, THEY DID NOT. As far as can be known, she never saw Charles Watkins again and seemingly never made an effort to communicate with him. Perhaps he was part of a life she was ready to leave behind her. An outbound train would lead her to a new future, a clean slate.

And as she stepped onto the train north, she disappeared from this story, evading any attempts (and there certainly must have been some) to bring her back to Virginia to testify in a courtroom. Neither the prosecutor nor the historian would ever know what she knew.

The Edith Friebel who departed Roanoke was much different than the frail, pitiable girl who had been jailed for her lover's crime. Far from "crazed with grief," she was bold, defiant and outspoken, perhaps hardened by her experience. Or perhaps she was never the wide-eyed victim of a charming paramour. Maybe she was a cunning woman who always tried to shape her own destiny. Things had not worked out with a certain Mr. Watkins of Virginia, to say the least. But she would move on.

Did she have anything to hide? Was she, in fact, an "accessory before or after the fact" to the murder of Susan Watkins? Note that, when asked on that last day in town where she was going, she, like a person not wanting to be traced, gave multiple answers: Cincinnati, Chicago, Milwaukee, finally settling on Harrisburg. And from there—no one would know. She, the only person besides Charles who could provide information to bring the full story to light, retreated to the shadows. If she was guilty of anything beyond poor judgment in her love life, she would face no consequences for it.

THE *ROANOKE TIMES* STORY of Ida's departure from Roanoke was notable for another reason: accompanying the story was the first appearance of a sketch of Charles Watkins. The artist was not identified, but it was presumably an accurate rendering. (Photos of Charles were found in Susan's trunks and may have served as source material.) It shows a handsome, confident man, well dressed, sporting fashionable muttonchop whiskers and a slightly receding hairline. The sketch would be used multiple times in coming months and even appeared once in the *Salem Times-Register*. Perhaps it graced wanted posters of the day as well. It is the only surviving image of the man.

By the time Ida Friebel disappeared from any official scrutiny, Charles Watkins had been on the run for two weeks. With each passing day, the chances of apprehending the fugitive were diminished. And the effort was hampered by what many thought a flaw in the system: local law enforcement had no funds for searching for fugitive suspects, and the state government was notoriously parsimonious when it came to such issues. As odd as it sounds to modern ears, the costs of hunting for a wanted man was expected to be borne by law enforcement personnel themselves.

Virginia governor Philip McKinney approved a $100 reward for catching Watkins—a considerable, but not overwhelming, sum for the day. But even having this reward approved took some ten days—during which Watkins proved to be long gone. While such a reward might be an incentive for

Charles Watkins.

Charles Watkins, from the contemporary *Roanoke Times* newspaper sketch. *Author's collection.*

someone to apprehend the wanted man, it did nothing before the fact to cover the personal costs of officers working the case.

On May 1, the *Salem Times-Register* quoted a local African American newspaper, the *Roanoke Weekly Press*. Speaking of the ongoing search for Watkins, the paper opined, "We think it a very bad arrangement on the part of the authorities not to have some definite understanding as to allowances to be made for the apprehension of criminals and fugitives from justice." The *Times-Register* agreed, urging other newspapers to take up the call for funds in such cases: "If there had been money which the county officers could have obtained immediately after the murder for telegraphing and detective work, [Watkins] would now have been in Salem jail."

Months later, on October 3, in coverage of another case with a missing suspect (Salem's Circus Murder, described later), the *Roanoke Times* noted that George Zirkle, by then Roanoke County sheriff, had spent $60.00 of his own money in the search for Watkins. It was money that would not be reimbursed by the Commonwealth of Virginia, Governor McKinney having stubbornly disallowed such an expenditure. "Funds for the arrest of escaping criminals have to come out of the pockets of private individuals…. This makes officials seem somewhat slow in these matters," noted the *Times* laconically. (Actually, it seems that Zirkle was reimbursed for at least some of his expenses, albeit by the local government, not the state. In the October 1891 minutes of the Roanoke County Board of Supervisors, a very precise amount of $34.61 was approved for "G.W. Zirkle, Sheriff, for special [expenses] in arresting Chas. Watkins." What expenditures were covered by this is unclear, nor is it known if the $60.00 mentioned by the *Roanoke Times* includes or is in addition to this appropriation.)

However, it might be noted that in the case of Watkins, local officials were anything but reluctant to carry on the search. In fact, they proved so eager that more than a few mistaken identifications—and even arrests—occurred over the spring and early summer of 1891.

LOCATING, IDENTIFYING AND APPREHENDING a fugitive suspect is today a routine matter for law enforcement. Instantaneous communication across the globe, fingerprint and DNA evidence, omnipresent cameras and widely accepted identity documents make it extraordinarily difficult to hide from authorities for long. But none of this existed in 1891. Even if the Roanoke County Sheriff's Office had the financial resources to pursue the subject, it would be a challenge to figure out if any given man of roughly the same age and appearance was, in fact, the fugitive Charles Watkins.

Watkins's physical description was nondistinctive enough—a midthirties, fair-skinned African American, tall with facial hair—that thousands of men could become suspects. It would be easy enough for him to melt into a crowd, change his name (and to a point his appearance) and begin life anew. There is no way of knowing how many wanted criminals did just that.

Photos of Watkins existed, found in Susan's trunks, and apparently these were disseminated, certainly a slow and laborious process in an age without fax machines and email. At the July 1891 session of the Roanoke County Board of Supervisors, an unusual expense request appeared on the docket alongside routine items such as medical care for paupers or road repairs by property owners. The Maury brothers, operators of a Salem photography studio, entered a request of eight dollars for providing photos of Charles Watkins. Such requests took some time to arrive on the agenda of the supervisors (who only met once or twice a month in those days of inactive local government). This suggests the photos had been taken sometime before, no doubt copied from Susan's originals, and utilized in the manhunt.

At the same time, given the racial conventions of the day and the award for Watkins's arrest, any black man who vaguely resembled the fugitive could find himself in unexpected and unjustified trouble. We know of several who did, and it's not impossible that several more such cases went unreported.

As related earlier, due to some sensationalistic journalism of the *Roanoke Herald*, rumors abounded (and persisted for several days) that Watkins had been arrested in Liberty, Bedford County. It is unclear if anyone had, in fact, been arrested or if the report was entirely false, but if someone was held in custody as Charles Watkins, he was soon released.

Only a week later, a second false rumor was reported, this time involving yet another Roanoke newspaper, the *World*, which also seemed to be questionable in the area of journalistic ethics. The *World*, eager to get a scoop, hired a private detective to hunt down the wanted man, and it was reported in both the *Roanoke Times* and the *Salem Times-Register* that an arrest had been made in Campbell County, Virginia. The detective hastily traveled east to Rustburg, the county seat, only to discover that the man in custody "did not resemble [Watkins] in the slightest degree." The *Roanoke Times*, poking some fun at its competitor, opined that the man would have good grounds to sue the detective for false arrest.

A man in Connellsville, Pennsylvania, was mistakenly arrested as Watkins in the aftermath of labor unrest and the infamous "Morewood Massacre," an incident near there. His name was not given, and presumably he was soon cleared of any involvement in the Watkins case. Even as late as June 5, there were still local sightings in the Roanoke Valley of the fugitive suspect. The *Times-Register* reported that an unnamed waiter from the Hotel Lucerne in Salem had been seen boarding a train in west Roanoke County and had been mistakenly identified as Watkins.

But the most significant case of mistaken identity, and the one that had the most risk of bringing an innocent man to trial, was the strange saga of Jacob Evans.

JACOB EVANS WAS BORN in Fincastle, Botetourt County, Virginia, probably sometime around the end of the Civil War. Like a lot of African Americans from rural regions around Roanoke, he must have seen opportunity awaiting in the railroad boomtown and moved there to seek his fortune. He found work in one of the hotels there, which is likely how he came to meet Charles Watkins. They formed a friendship, perhaps one cemented by the odd coincidence that they bore a striking resemblance to each other. It seems that Jacob also struck up a friendship with Charles's cousin Addie Anderson, who also worked for various hotels in Roanoke.

Sometime about 1890, Evans left the hotel business and took a job at a company store for the Crozier Iron Furnace along the railroad tracks. He stayed there for some months but, in early January 1891, decided to move north to Pittsburg, Pennsylvania (as the city's name was spelled at that time, the terminal *h* having been officially, if temporarily, dropped). By February, he had obtained employment at the store of Posey and Kerr on Federal Street, working long hours with little time off and seemingly doing a good job of it.

Exactly what happened to draw the law's attention to Jacob Evans is unclear, but the *Pittsburg Dispatch* suggested that visitors from the Roanoke Valley chanced to see Evans in Pittsburg, misidentified him as Charles Watkins and, upon their return, informed Henry Webber of their suspicions. Webber, brother of the soon-to-retire sheriff of Roanoke County, was a bootmaker by trade but also served as a deputy for his brother and, on the side, would run his own detective agency. In a day when professional law enforcement had little investigative power and scant resources to pursue fugitive suspects, such detective firms often filled those niches.

Investigate Webber did, thoroughly and meticulously. Addie Anderson, cousin of Charles Watkins, was at the time employed as a servant in the home of Alexander Asberry, the postmaster of Roanoke. One day, Asberry, no doubt at the behest of Henry Webber, approached Addie and asked what she knew of a Jacob Evans and his current whereabouts. Perhaps a bit nonplussed at the questioning, she replied that she had known him once but that he had left town and that the last letter she'd received from him was postmarked Pittsburg. Sometime later, Asberry again approached Addie as she worked and informed her that the man she thought was Jacob Evans was indeed her cousin, having assumed that name to escape justice. Addie was probably secretly amused at the suggestion, knowing better than her employer who was or was not her cousin. But she did not contradict Asberry.

Though nothing in the historical record indicates Henry Webber personally traveled to Pennsylvania, it's not impossible that he did, ascertaining that a man matching the suspect's description was indeed in Pittsburg, learning exactly where he worked and concluding that he reasonably could be assumed to be Watkins, living under the assumed name of his doppelganger from Virginia.

Accordingly, in late May 1891, Webber began a lengthy correspondence, by telegraph and mail, with Police Superintendent Henry Muth of Allegheny County, Pennsylvania. Webber shared the results of his investigation, a description of the crime and of the suspect's known habits, and a photograph of Charles Watkins. Finally, Webber issued a formal warrant for the arrest of Charles Watkins, alias Jacob Evans. While the authorities in Pittsburg seemed to have their doubts, they had no choice but to have Evans arrested. Two officers named Steele and Johnson were sent to arrest Jacob Evans on May 29.

Not surprisingly, and at first not convincingly, Evans protested his complete innocence. He was not Charles Watkins, though he had known the man in Virginia and was aware from the national coverage of the crime in newspapers that he was a wanted man. But he had murdered no one, Evans insisted, certainly aware that the criminal justice system had an intrinsic bias against his race and that more than a few men had faced the noose on less tenuous identifications.

But fortunately for Evans, it did not take long for Henry Webber's carefully crafted investigation to begin to unravel.

Evans's employer, George Kerr, personally came to the jail to visit the suspect. He gladly and convincingly provided an airtight alibi. Jacob Evans, he informed the authorities, had been in Pittsburg and working at his store every day (except for one half day off) since February, so he could not possibly have been responsible for a murder in Roanoke County, Virginia, in April. Many of his customers could vouch for the same timeline. "Whether Evans is Watkins or merely himself and nobody else, he can prove a very capital alibi," admitted the *Dispatch*.

Another flurry of telegraphs between Muth and Webber ensued. Webber, no doubt, was disappointed that he had not caught his man, but he could not, in the face of this new and reliable evidence, continue to insist that Evans was Watkins. He canceled the warrant and told Muth to release the man, guilty of nothing but looking remarkably like a wanted murderer.

Evans was magnanimous about the affair and judicious in choosing not to be too critical of the authorities in either location. "I am not so ignorant," he told the *Dispatch*, "as to blame the officers for arresting me. When a murder has been committed and a man is suspected, he must be arrested." He walked out of the jail to his freedom and faded from the historical record.

Too many innocent men had been suspected of being Charles Watkins, but the fugitive as still at large. The trail to apprehend the murderer of Susan Watkins grew cold. All of the false sightings and mistaken identities were, however, about to come to an end. The real man would soon be arrested. And he would have no one to blame but himself.

6

"YOUR MAN WATKINS IN JAIL HERE, AWAITING PROPER PAPERS"

The sun was a fiery orange disk sinking into the west as Ben Wright settled into the cane chair on the porch. This was his favorite time of day; after a hard day's work and a plain but satisfying meal with his family, he relished the chance to sit his weary bones down, light a pipe and enjoy the last hour of twilight. The younger children were running around playing something noisy with other neighborhood children; he recalled the exuberance of his own childhood with a smile. Laura, his oldest, sat across the street with some other neighborhood girls her age, no doubt swapping gossip and giggling over the antics of boys.

Ben nodded to a few passersby, all black of course. White folks almost never ventured down this street, although of necessity Ben and his neighbors frequently went in and out of the white residential streets. Blacksmithing kept him at his forge most of the day, but there were occasions to deliver a repaired andiron here or a cask of nails there. Ben reckoned he knew most of the folks in town, black and white.

Salem was, after all, a small community, and while there were several blacksmiths sweating over forges in the town, he was one of the busiest. It seemed like he'd shoed most of the horses he saw along the street at one time or another; he'd provided nails or hinges or other hardware for many of the buildings that had mushroomed up in town during the recent boom years. He had the respect of his neighbors on both sides of Main Street, he reflected with a bit of pride. He worked hard and earned a stable living for Mary and the children.

Of course, he was a black man in a white man's world, and like all his neighbors he keenly felt the pressure to keep his place. He had a lot to defend in his comfortable life, and even an inauspicious comment to the wrong person could bring trouble. Like most men of his race, he didn't speak his mind except in safe surroundings.

Still, he felt inordinately secure on that pleasant evening. He even allowed himself to think that the ugliness about his cousin was past. To be sure, Charles was still at large, and the crime was not resolved. He thought back often to the evening he and Mary had spent with that lady named Susan, how he offered to accompany her to find her wayward husband that spring Sunday afternoon. He'd done what he felt he had to do. There was no way, he told himself for the umpteenth time, that he could have known he was delivering her to her death.

Ben was not responsible. Charles was. Simple as that. Yet every time he thought of Susan Watkins, lying in that unmarked grave up on the hill, he felt pangs of regret. What had happened to her, dying alone in that cold creek, betrayed by the man who once swore to love her—it wasn't right. Ben had known Charles his whole life and had always liked his personable cousin. But no one should get away with murder.

Laura suddenly dashed across the street and into the doorway, reappearing only a moment later. "Pa, I forgot. I picked up a letter for you at the post office." She handed him an envelope and ran back across the street to her girlfriends. Ben called his thanks after her and looked down at the envelope—from a Williams. He couldn't recall any Williams he knew out of town. The postmark was smeared and hard to read in the failing light, but it was somewhere in North Carolina. Curious. He checked the address to be sure it wasn't misdelivered, but sure enough, it said Ben Wright, Salem, Virginia. Something about the handwriting seemed…

Ben froze, felt his heart skip a beat. For a solitary moment, he considered taking the letter to the cookstove and throwing it in unopened. He knew the handwriting, and he vividly recalled the last time he'd seen it. It was what had convinced him all those weeks ago that the stranger from Milwaukee was telling the truth about his cousin. Part of him, a big part, wanted nothing to do with this letter. Whatever it said, it could only be trouble.

He stared at it for a few more minutes, long enough that Mary noticed his odd behavior through the door. She'd been curious about the letter since Laura brought it home. "Ben, what is it? You look like you've seen a ghost."

"Nothing," he muttered. "Leave me be." He stood and walked out to the street. Taking his pocketknife out, he slit the envelope open and took out the letter, heart pounding, turning so the setting sun illuminated the page. "Dear Cousin Ben: I know that you are my friend if there is anyone on earth…"

Ben read on, at times shocked and at times infuriated. I was the cause of it? He forgives *me*? Not a cursing man by habit, Ben let slip a few choice words, thankful the children were out of earshot.

And that one line. There was no other way to interpret it. It was a confession, clear as day.

Mary joined him on the street. "You gonna tell me about it?"

"We're going to burn this letter right now and forget we ever saw it." Ben said. After all, the letter instructed him to do just that. But instead, he handed it to Mary, forgetting for a moment that his wife had never learned to read much. She looked at him quizzically. He took the letter back and read it to her. Her hands went to her mouth in shock as she listened.

"What do I do with this?" Ben asked the person in the world he trusted the most. He knew what he held in his still-quivering hand: vital evidence in an unsolved criminal case. But turning it over to the law was tantamount to betraying a relative. He couldn't condone murder, not at all, even within the family. But folks of his skin color had good reason to steer clear of law enforcement.

Mary had always been his conscience. She didn't hesitate. "You know what you have to do. You take that letter straight to the law in the morning. I don't care if it was from your own mother. You ain't gonna bear false witness." It was the same thing she had told him several times last April when he was called to testify to the coroner's jury.

Ben knew she was right. He'd go see Henry Webber first thing. He folded the letter into the envelope and went back into the house, already knowing it would be a sleepless night. But tomorrow night, he would sleep with a clean conscience.[22]

By summer, the search for Charles Watkins had largely faded from public awareness in the Roanoke Valley. News reports on Watkins, absent any breaks in the case, had disappeared from the papers. Since the mistaken identity debacle surrounding Jacob Evans, law enforcement seemed to be out of leads. If people were discussing the case, the conversation probably revolved around the dimming chances of apprehending the fugitive.

There was one change in the dramatis personae of the case effective July 1. Sheriff Charles Webber retired, having declined to run for reelection. As he was popular and respected, his departure from office was lamented by the editor of the *Salem Times-Register*, a paper of which Webber had been a founder and his brother edited: "[A] faithful and efficient officer…[his retirement] was a subject of general regret with the voters of his county."

Webber was replaced by the newly elected George W. Zirkle, who would hold the title until 1908. A Confederate veteran (he had served in the storied Salem Flying Artillery, reputed to have fired the "last shot" of Lee's army at Appomattox), Zirkle was a former deputy sheriff. His experience and calm demeanor would serve him well in office. He also had a familiarity with the most-wanted fugitive he had inherited. As a child, Charles Watkins had lived on Zirkle's farm, and Zirkle had helped him get some measure of education at the Gum Spring school. Now it was his job to apprehend him and likely deliver him to the gallows

Sheriff Charles Webber. *Salem Historical Society.*

At the same time Charles Webber retired, his brother Henry ceased to be deputy sheriff, replaced by one J.H. Hening.[23] Henry Webber, however, did not abandon the search for Charles Watkins, but continued to pursue leads as a private investigator. "People here had almost forgotten the matter," noted the *Salem Times-Register*. But "not so Detective Henry Webber."

His diligence in pursuing Watkins is all the more impressive given that Henry had, on June 25, lost his wife of seven years to the hazards of childbirth, as well as the son she was delivering. Perhaps the pursuit of justice was a means to assuage his grief.

So where was the elusive Charles Watkins?

Unbeknownst to anyone, Watkins had made his way to the coast of North Carolina and assumed a new identity: Samuel G. Williams. As previously described, he gave two accounts of his venture there, a trek of nearly three hundred miles. In one, he made a leisurely railroad journey, in another, an impoverished "foot-walk" that nearly killed him.

Yet somehow, upon arrival in New Hanover County, North Carolina, Watkins/Williams was able to procure a job as a waiter at the Island Beach Hotel on a barrier island known as the Hammocks, near Wrightsville Beach.

How a bedraggled fugitive, unable to provide references or any verifiable backstory, who presumably had not bathed, shaved or changed clothes for days, was able to be hired at an elegant resort is not known, but it testifies to the charm evinced by the man. Only a man of supreme self-confidence and acting ability could have pulled off such a feat. Furthermore, he was not only hired but also soon promoted to the important and visible position of head waiter.

As head waiter, Watkins was a crucial figure at the Island Beach Hotel. His duties required him to supervise the other waiters, meet the needs of the guests and act as a liaison between the white management and the African American staff. A sense of his duties and the importance of his position might be gleaned from a 1904 book titled *Commanders of the Dining-Room*:

> [The head waiter] *stands at the dining room door as the vice host, receiving the guests, paying extra honors to distinguished patrons as they enter, and at the same time surveying the dining room, seeing that everything in this department is moving in regular order, and is in keeping with the high standard of the house, diplomatically pacifying patrons with real or imaginary grievances, and maintaining proper order in the dining room, among a large number of men, who are under his supervision....* [He] *is selected because he possesses all the qualifications that are necessary to fill these various high positions that are combined under the common title "head waiter."* [24]

Charles, now Sam Williams, excelled at the job. He was once again in his milieu. He spent his days indoors dressed in finery, he ate well and slept in a comfortable bed, his pay was more generous than a former slave could usually expect in the South, appreciative white customers complimented him on his work and gave him generous tips. No one could guess the truth behind the amiable waiter.

But it's not hard to imagine that a storm brewed beneath his calm and proper demeanor, a storm of guilt and regret mixed with fear and apprehension. He had killed one wife and abandoned the other; he had turned his back on all family and friends to escape justice. For the moment, he was safe from detection, but how long could that last? There is no way of knowing how aware he was of the manhunt being carried out in Virginia or the suspicions surrounding Jacob Evans, but in unguarded moments, he no doubt looked over his shoulder. How long before the ghosts of his past caught up with him? Near his new home, Charles would later mention, there were fifteen or twenty thousand soldiers stationed. At least a few were from southwest Virginia. Every day, Charles must have expected to be recognized by someone and arrested, and when it finally happened, he claimed a feeling of relief.

He could pretend to be Sam Williams, but he could not escape being Charles Watkins.

Perhaps it isn't surprising that Watkins felt trapped in his successful masquerade, and any trapped creature envisions a route of escape. Each morning, Charles could look across at the Atlantic Ocean, smell the sea breezes, see oceangoing vessels crossing the waves. On days off, perhaps he strolled the beach and looked eastward beyond the horizon—Europe was there. In his career serving white people in fancy hotels, Charles had no doubt met many Europeans and many Americans who had visited the Old Country—he even once claimed to speak some German, perhaps learned from Edith. In Europe, he knew, men and women of his skin color were treated better, were not as segregated, could even intermarry. In Europe, no one had ever heard of Charles and Susan Watkins. There was his escape route: he would go to Europe, perhaps work his way across on a passenger ship and get a job in a hotel in London or Paris or Nice.

But that had to be in the future. He had to save money, wait for opportunities to open. For now, he had to be Sam Williams the head waiter. But that couldn't stop the gnaw of remorse. How did it come to this? Who was to blame? As his stressed mind mulled the events of the previous April, he settled on a villain to the story, a single culprit for ruining his life.

His cousin Ben Wright. It was all Ben's fault.

Ben had brought that woman to Roanoke, right to his door. Ben had set in motion a chain of events that turned him into Sam Williams, tore Ida from his life and left Susan dead in a creek. Ben lived happily with his family in his hometown, while Charles was in exile. Ben was to blame, and one day Charles simply had to let him know that. He wrote Ben a letter—the "fatal letter," the papers would soon call it.

Dated July 4, from nearby Wilmington, Watkins's letter gives a glimpse into the tortured mind of Sam Williams, fugitive wife murderer. Among the facts that can be deduced from the epistle: Charles did not know where Ida was, he considered Susan a threat to his and Ida's life and he regretted abandoning Ida to her fate. In this letter, he clearly exonerated himself from any wrongdoing—he had only done what he had to do. But most importantly for authorities, it revealed his alias and his location.

And the letter, significantly, contained an unmistakable confession of murder. When Charles stamped that letter to Ben, he sealed his own fate.

BEN WRIGHT RECEIVED THE letter from his cousin on July 13 and turned it over to Henry Webber in Salem the next day. Webber was no longer a deputy, but he wanted justice done and to see the case resolved. Webber immediately informed newly installed sheriff, George Zirkle.

There was work to do, a procedure to follow. Webber and Zirkle needed to confirm the facts suggested by the letter, and they had to get the authority to bring the suspect to Virginia if it all panned out—if this wasn't another Jacob Evans episode.

By Friday, they had telegraphed Colonel E.D. Hall, chief of police for New Hanover County, North Carolina. Hall promised to investigate and confirmed that a warrant from the governor of Virginia would be necessary for an extradition.

Chief Hall assigned two of his best men, officers Ben Turlington and Bob Green, to follow the leads. They needed to identify "Sam Williams" conclusively and then be sure he was in fact Charles Watkins. No doubt a physical description was dispatched via telegraph, and a copy of the photograph of Watkins was sent.

Turlington and Green invented a ruse to be sure which African American waiter was Williams. They informed the hotel management that a letter for S.G. Williams was awaiting him at the post office; then they sat to observe. When Williams picked up the letter (exactly what it contained was never revealed), they trailed him to the Island Beach Hotel at the Hammocks. Turlington then began an observation in the hotel under the guise of a fisherman seeking to sell his catch of softshell crabs to the kitchen. Surreptitiously, Turlington observed the head waiter. The man certainly matched the description, and he bore an identifying mark beyond dispute.

While in custody, Ida Friebel revealed that she had once made for Charles a pair of embroidered suspenders. Carefully wrought on them were pansies and daisies in silk thread and the initials of the man Ida loved: *C* on one strap, *W* on the other. How Sam Williams explained the monogram is not known, but the unmistakable accoutrement confirmed for Turlington that he was indeed Charles Watkins, fugitive wife killer.

Officer Turlington reported back that they had their man and received the go-ahead for the arrest. On the evening of Sunday, July 19, Charles Watkins sat down to a dinner of beefsteak in his room at the Island Beach Hotel. Hearing a knock at the door, he opened it to find Chief Hall and Turlington and Green there to arrest him. Calmly, he noted their drawn pistols and told them weapons were unnecessary, that he would go quietly with them. He further asked if he could sit down and finish his steak before departing. This request was denied, and Charles Watkins was quietly taken into custody, with no attempt to resist arrest.

It had been 104 days since Susan Watkins had breathed her last.

Watkins's arrest in North Carolina did not conclude the case, of course. The New Hanover County sheriff dutifully telegraphed Zirkle and Webber: "Your man Watkins in jail here, awaiting proper papers." The obvious next step, in other words, would be to bring him back to Virginia to stand trial, and for that, Chief Hall informed Webber, he would have to have a warrant from the governor of Virginia to extradite the prisoner.

As luck would have it, Governor Phillip McKinney was in the neighborhood of Roanoke, vacationing at the nearby Blue Ridge Springs resort. Only a short rail trip for Sheriff Zirkle and Detective Webber, this allowed them to call personally on the governor and hopefully save the time it would take to travel to Richmond. McKinney was certainly amenable to the extradition but informed the two lawmen that a warrant still had to be arranged through the secretary of state at the capitol. Accordingly, Webber departed immediately for Richmond, while Sheriff Zirkle made arrangements to travel to Wilmington, where Watkins was being held. Webber agreed to meet him there with the paperwork in order.

Meanwhile, Charles spent his week in a North Carolina jail. Some of the African American acquaintances he'd made locally came to visit him, bringing him fruit to eat. Even his employer from the Island Beach Hotel called, professing his belief in Charles's innocence and offering to assist him with legal counsel. When visitors asked him about the charges against him, he acknowledged that he had been named in a warrant but refused to talk about the specific accusation. He likely fooled no one; his story had been featured prominently in the Wilmington papers.

News of the arrest hit the Roanoke papers on Tuesday, July 21: "Charles Watkins Captured" read the front-page headline of the *Roanoke Times*. The case had faded so far from public memory that the story mistakenly confused Susan with Lucy Watkins. It seems that the reporter was aware that a letter had exposed Watkins's location, and even had some awareness of the contents of the missive (such as Charles's plan to immigrate to Europe). However, the paper initially believed the letter was sent to his cousin Addie Anderson and was only one of several such correspondences. If indeed Charles wrote more than one letter to his relations in Virginia, only the one was ever entered into evidence at his trial.

"The Villain Caught!" proclaimed the weekly *Salem Times-Register* on Friday, July 24. Recounting the details of the case, the paper also noted that the lynching threats of months ago had diminished:

> *The general satisfaction over his capture is such that we have no idea anything of the kind would be attempted now. Once safely in the hands of the law his punishment is certain, and if there should be a disposition on the part of any of our people, either white or colored, to take the law in their own hands, we urge them to abandon it, and allow the law to take its course.*

The *Roanoke Times* agreed, noting the same day that "there is no excitement among the negroes over the matter. They want to see Watkins get a fair showing in the courts, but think he stands a poor chance." The arrival of Webber and Zirkle with their prisoner was expected on Friday, but it was Saturday when the train carrying them pulled into the Roanoke depot.

As soon as the 6:10 p.m. train came to a stop, a flood of curious onlookers rushed into the smoking car to see the famed fugitive. Webber (apparently Sheriff Zirkle was content to consider him in charge of the prisoner) saw no harm in satiating the curiosity of the crowd. And for his part, Charles ate up the attention, his moment of celebrity.

Charles Watkins was, if anything, an actor. He knew how to play a role, to do what was expected of him in a given situation, to draw much-desired attention to himself. To his family at home, he could be a slave-born native of a small Virginia town. If he was a servant in a prestigious hotel, he was suave and debonair. To a starry-eyed girl from rural Wisconsin, he could turn on the charm and win her heart. He could walk into a coastal hotel as a total stranger and talk himself into a job. Now he would perform for the curious crowd and the local press a new role: innocent victim of a great misunderstanding.

Webber invited acquaintances of the suspect to call on him briefly; several, white and black, availed themselves of the opportunity. Some offered him sandwiches and cigars, but Charles declined. A larger crowd, however, was outside on the platform, and Webber suggested that Watkins raise the shade and let them have a glimpse as well.

Charles recognized some of his former coworkers from the Hotel Felix in the crowd and conversed with them for a few minutes, joking that the sea air and seafood diet of coastal Carolina had agreed with his health. The proprietor of the Felix spoke to a *Times* reporter, as did past guests who had known Watkins months before. Some expressed faith in Charles's innocence.

After a few more minutes, the train's gong sounded, indicating that it would soon depart the station. The next stop would be Salem, only a few minutes west. A reporter for the *Roanoke Times* tagged along—unnamed in the press account, but perhaps Frank Lovelock. Charles, in his element, spoke freely about his recent experiences, praising Webber and Zirkle for their humane treatment. He described his flight to Carolina back in April but was too astute to say anything of material relevance to the accusation against him, except to assert his innocence of the "grave charges" that faced him. Was he putting on an act? Or did he really believe that a trial would go in his favor?

As the train neared Salem, Watkins's sunny disposition suddenly chilled. He was aware, perhaps from Webber, that threats of lynching had been made against him months earlier. What awaited him at the Salem depot?

Zirkle assured him that he was determined to protect his prisoner from any violence, and a relieved Watkins held up his hands for Detective Webber to place him in handcuffs as the train came to a stop. (Up to this point his legs had been shackled, but his hands were free.)

Salem's passenger rail depot about 1891. *Salem Historical Society.*

As it turned out, there were few people awaiting the train at the depot, and the two lawmen easily moved their prisoner to a waiting omnibus borrowed from the Hotel Lucerne. However, they encountered a crowd as they proceeded up College Avenue to the jail beside the courthouse. Many in the crowd, described as mostly black, followed the omnibus up College, but peacefully. Salem's African American community wanted to see the prisoner in jail, not lynched, prior accusations to the contrary notwithstanding. The only interaction Charles had with the onlookers was to accept a cigarette and a light from one gentleman.

Arriving at the jail, Charles was quickly and uneventfully led inside. "As the bolt shot into the socket, the crowd cheered loudly and dispersed," the *Times* reported. For his part, Watkins breathed a sigh of relief to be out of the reach of anyone who would do him immediate harm. Deputy sheriff and jailer J.H. Hening removed the shackles and allowed him to rest a while before confining him in his cell. Charles Watkins, fugitive and accused wife killer, was back.

And the Roanoke County jail would be his abode for the rest of his life.

ON MONDAY, CHARLES SPOKE again (through the window of his cell) with an unnamed reporter from the *Roanoke Times*. Whether it was the same one who accompanied him on the train is unclear, but the reporter had an obviously high degree of familiarity with the details of Watkins's case, so it may well have been Lovelock, who had served on the coroner's jury three months before.

The writer describes Watkins as haggard, with "an uneasy look plainly noticeable in his eyes." Indeed, the prisoner twice proclaimed that his "brain was troubled" by his situation, but he expressed confidence that he would "get out of this trouble." Charles had no complaints about his cell or his treatment in the county jail but seemed disappointed that he had had only one visitor since arriving—an unnamed cousin from Roanoke, perhaps Addie Anderson. When he spoke of his case, he expressed utmost confidence in exoneration. He brashly proclaimed that he would hire Colonel George Hansbrough as his attorney. Not only was Hansbrough a former employer of Charles's from his days as a farmhand in west Roanoke County, but he also was the same lawyer who had negotiated Ida's release weeks before (although it is uncertain if Charles was aware of this fact). To assist Hansbrough, he planned to hire A.B. Pugh, calling him "one of the sharpest young lawyers about here."

In response to questions from the reporter, Charles asserted that he did not know the location of Ida Friebel but presumed she had returned to Wisconsin. He denied rumors that it had taken six men to arrest him and that he had attempted to escape from the train en route to Virginia.

At an incidental mention of Susan's name, Charles suddenly asked the reporter if any money had been found on the body. The reporter accurately replied that she was found with some jewelry but no cash; this elicited a long sigh from the prisoner, seemingly surprised that there was no money discovered with the corpse. Tellingly calling Susan "my wife," Watkins spoke of her (and his) expensive tastes in clothing and adornments.

Asked about witnesses, Charles immediately said he would need call only two but did not describe who or what their testimony would be. It seems he was trying his own case in his mind, with no bearing on reality. He also denied writing any letters home while in North Carolina, maintaining he had only written inquiries to various merchants in the north about apparel.

His denial of "the fatal letter" is understandable—it would be damning evidence against him in court. But could it be he actually did not recall the letter to Ben Wright? Did he compose and mail it in an unbalanced frame of mind or a state of intoxication?

A few days later, Watkins spoke to another reporter, from the *Salem Times-Register*. Much of what he said parallels the earlier interview, but there were some new revelations. For one, he implied that the *Roanoke Times* interview had misquoted or misrepresented him on several points.

He also revealed that he'd met with attorneys Hansbrough and Pugh, who told him what they no doubt would have said any other defendant: they would happily defend him if he could raise the necessary money. As it would transpire, Hansbrough would have only a minor association with Watkins's defense at his arraignment. Pugh would serve as lead counsel, although how Charles intended to pay for his services, and that of his partners, is unclear.

"He does not really seem to comprehend the seriousness of the charge against him," noted the *Times-Register* reporter. "Or if he does, he holds out a very bold front regarding it." If Charles Watkins was to some degree in a state of denial, he was aware enough of his situation to avoid incriminating himself. Both writers to interview him noted how carefully he avoided discussing the charges or the material evidence against him. His brain may have been troubled, but he was too smart to reveal any secrets that could be used by the coming prosecution.

The reporter asked Charles the reason for having changed his name to Sam Williams while a fugitive. His answer was a bit nonsensical: "I principally changed my name because as head waiter everyone gets on to your name, and I did not want the name of Charles Watkins connected with me in my position." He added by way of explanation that "the day I went to the Hammocks my name was mentioned in the papers." If his assuming an alias was not necessarily an admission of guilt, it certainly reflected the inescapable fact that a shadow lay across the name of Charles Watkins.

The prisoner again denied having written any incriminating letter but would say little on the subject except that "that will be better known afterwards." He again spoke of his disappointment in the lack of support from his former neighbors in Salem and the west county. "A few colored friends from Roanoke and Lynchburg have been to see me, but colored people come round and ask you how you are, but can't do much else. The colored people here are down on me very much. I don't think that the colored people of Salem ought to have such malice against me until they have heard both sides."

But in contrast Charles noted that "the white folks are really the only friends I have; they will stand by me; the whites have been my friends since I was a boy and went to school at Gum Spring." He claimed, rather implausibly, that some forty white friends from as far away as Baltimore had come to visit him since his incarceration in Salem.

Actually, he was overly optimistic about his public support. As the court proceedings and resultant press coverage would show, there seemed to be

Roanoke County Courthouse. The roof and chimney behind the wing on the left is the county jail. *Salem Historical Society.*

very few people, white or black, who were on his side. His guilt seemed to be a foregone conclusion in both the press and public opinion.

But public opinion was beside the point. It would be in a courtroom where his fate would be decided, an unexpectedly long process destined to involve months of legal wrangling. And in the court of law, Charles Watkins enjoyed one decided advantage: he was innocent until proven guilty beyond a reasonable doubt.

"THIS IS A MIGHTY SLOW PROCESS"

I moved here to slow down, thought Arthur Benton Pugh. So why am I always in such a hurry?

Pugh did slow down, if only momentarily, to cross Main Street. Caution was always a prudent thing on Main. Between the occasional streetcar and the omnipresent horses and wagons, there were more than a few accidents in bustling Salem. And of course, even if traffic was light, there were always things into which it would be better not to step before standing before a judge in court.

He crossed safely to the courthouse lawn and paused a moment in the shade of the bandstand to catch his breath and collect his thoughts. Too busy, too busy, he thought. But it's better to be busy than bored, he reminded himself—especially since bored never pays the bills.

This time last year, money was not a consideration in his life. He was an up-and-coming attorney with the Department of the Interior in Washington, D.C., and making a good living—perhaps not the richest attorney in town, but his position was secure. As railroads continued to cross the continent, land claims and the intricacies of the general land laws of the United States were complex enough to keep a flock of lawyers engaged. Pugh found the work challenging and steady, but the pressure was considerable. Official life in the nation's capital was simply not suited to my tastes, he decided at last.

He'd heard of Salem from a colleague who had passed through the pretty valley and spoke glowingly of the small town next to a booming railroad city. To Pugh, his description brought back memories of his West Virginia home, and surely a bright and talented lawyer could hang his shingle and make a living in such a place. And the slower, small-town pace of life was appealing to his lovely bride.

And so they'd moved to Roanoke County, and soon Pugh (with a bit of judicious self-promotion) found his new practice filling as many hours as his government job had. He was again up-and-coming and could choose to turn down cases when he decided, taking only the cases that seemed most lucrative and interesting.

And yet, his hurry this morning was for a case he was almost certain to lose and couldn't possibly pay him anything for his trouble. Defending this murderer—accused murderer, he hastened to add, even in his own thoughts—was, in a sense, the right thing to do. The man seemed to be in a dream world of denial, unable to help himself, unaware of the severity of his position. More than many defendants he'd met, he needed competent representation. Even a colored man accused of wife-murder had rights, and the system depended on them being defended.

The man needed an attorney, and Pugh was a good one—very good. It wasn't about money, unlike some cases he took. His client would likely never pay him anything. It was about procedure.

Because, of course, all his legal training had taught him that a court trial was based on evidence. The prosecutor's job was to summon and present all the facts, all the testimony, that pointed to the defendant's guilt. They were considerable, Pugh had to admit.

But they weren't alone. The defense had the job of presenting the facts and skillfully interpreting them, which pointed to his client's innocence—or at least cast doubt on the certainty of his guilt. It was often the tougher job, but an essential one. And if Pugh did it well, it would bolster his reputation and build his practice, even if it ended up a losing cause.

The attorney had no illusions. This story would very likely end with his client on the gallows. But if so, there would be a spirited fight in the middle chapters. Arthur Pugh mopped his forehead with his handkerchief, gathered himself and strode confidently into the courthouse.

THE JUDICIAL JOURNEY THAT would decide the fate of Charles Watkins began with an anticlimactic formality. On July 28, three days after Watkins's arrival in the Roanoke County jail, deputy sheriff and jailer J.H. Hening accompanied one of the county's justices of the peace, John H. Camper, to the accused's cell. Camper, it will be recalled, was the official who presided over the coroner's inquest the previous April, the process that first collected evidence and witness testimony against the defendant. Camper's purpose was to conduct an examination of the prisoner, a preliminary investigation for the purpose of officially establishing that there was probable cause to conclude that a crime had been committed by a suspect in custody.

Camper's effort would have been an easy task in any event, there being no doubt that Susan Watkins was the victim of foul play, nor that Charles was indisputably the prime suspect. But Camper was saved even this minimal effort when Charles waived the examination. At this point, Charles had not yet retained counsel, so this could only be a decision he made on his own. The sole clue he gave for his reason was a cryptic comment that he thought it "best to keep the excitement down."

Waiving examination was not at all uncommon for defendants, and while it was nothing like an admission of guilt, it was generally a tacit acknowledgement that there was sufficient evidence for a prosecutor to take the case to court. In this case, waiving examination also seemed to give Watkins a choice of the court in which his trial would be held: Roanoke County's circuit court (presided over by Judge Henry Blair) or the county court, the Honorable Wingfield Griffin presiding. For reasons never explained, Watkins would choose the county court. He had claimed earlier to have had an acquaintance with Griffin years before; perhaps he hoped (vainly, as it would turn out) to receive more sympathy before his bench.

With this formality out of the way, the Commonwealth of Virginia summoned a grand jury to meet on Friday, July 31 to hear the evidence.

Public interest in the Watkins case continued to be high. Gossip and rumors were apparently flying through Roanoke City and County and occasionally filtered their way into the headlines. On the thirtieth, the *Roanoke Times* ran a front-page story on Addie Anderson, Charles's cousin. The story was short on established fact but long on gossip about the case.

The *Times* reporter, as usual unidentified, speculated that the "fatal letter" that had led to Charles's arrest had been addressed to Addie. Although some details about the letter had been leaked to the press, including that the recipient was a cousin, so far it seems only a handful of officials had seen the full contents. In fact, the story refers to "letters" in the plural, unclear about even the number.

The reporter spent some time tracking down Addie, briefly pursuing a completely unrelated woman of the same name, before finding the correct Miss Anderson. Appearing to the reporter as "troubled deeply" by her cousin's arrest, Addie quickly denied receiving any mail from the fugitive: "If Charles Watkins ever wrote to me after he left Roanoke, I never received the letter." But she claimed that a letter from someone had been sent to her, in care of an African American constable, a letter that had been intercepted and kept from her despite repeated requests for it. If such a letter actually existed, no other mention of it was ever made, and it may have been a completely incorrect assumption on her part. Indeed, when Henry Webber was queried by the reporter after the interview with Addie, he responded by stating (presumably truthfully) he knew nothing of a letter to Anderson, carefully and cannily failing to reveal that Ben Wright was the addressee in question.

The next day, the *Times* ran a sort of retraction, stating in passing that the letter revealing Charles to be Sam Williams was addressed in fact to an as then unnamed male. The previous story had mentioned an effort to get the $100 reward money for Watkins's arrest for Addie, which naturally went nowhere after this revelation. In fact, no record exists of who, if anyone, did receive that money. Arguably, Ben Wright may have had the strongest claim to it, although it may have gone to Henry Webber, if it was ever disbursed at all.

To the modern observer, court cases in nineteenth-century Virginia moved astonishingly quickly. Even for capital offenses, it was not unusual for a defendant to be tried, sentenced and executed within weeks of the actual crime. Charles Watkins's trial began nearly four months after Susan's murder, and the court proceedings would take much longer still—much to the frustration of many observers.

On July 31, a grand jury of eight men convened in Salem, in Judge Wingfield Griffin's county court, to consider the evidence against Watkins and decide whether there was sufficient evidence to indict him with a crime or crimes. D. Terry Martin, a prominent farmer and businessman from West Roanoke County, was selected as foreman, with Elias Murry, William Cook, James Stoutamire, Benjamin Trevey, James Barnett, W.O. Ferguson and Marshall P. Frantz filling the other jury slots. In an upstairs room at the Roanoke County Courthouse no doubt stifling with the summer heat, the panel heard from Fannie Coxe, Lucy Watkins (but not Taylor), Mat Bailey and Ben Wright, as well as Dr. Saunders, the physician who had examined Susan's remains for the coroner's inquest. The paper reported that an Asa Huff also testified; it seems likely that the reporter erred in the last name and it was instead Asa Jackson, an

African American neighbor who would testify at the later trial that he saw a man resembling Charles Watkins with a woman in the vicinity of the murder scene that fateful morning in April.

While the grand jury proceedings were not public—hence no testimony survives—it's not hard to imagine what these witnesses told the panel: Susan Watkins had been killed and Charles Watkins was the man who had motive, means and opportunity to commit the crime. Testimony continued for a little over an hour, so each witness had less than ten minutes to answer questions from Commonwealth's Attorney William Ballard.

While the jury deliberated, the *Roanoke Times* noted that "a large crowd had assembled in the courthouse, the Negroes predominating, manifesting a subdued but intense interest in everything relating to the case against Watkins." The left-hand side of the courtroom (reserved for African Americans in the segregated community, "according to long-established custom") was filled beyond capacity, with many standing.

Silence fell in the courtroom as the grand jury came downstairs and presented to Clerk of Court William McCauley its decision. McCauley read to Judge Griffin a document titled "Commonwealth vs. Charles Watkins: Indictment for murder. A true bill." The indictment came, certainly, as scant surprise to a community largely already convinced of Watkins's guilt.

William McCauley, clerk of court and local historian. *Salem Historical Society.*

The next step was an arraignment, but other matters intervened on the court's docket. An E.E. Walton was indicted for the felonious theft of a horse and carriage, and a complicated case of embezzlement was continued until the next session. As that defendant was led from the courtroom back to the nearby jail, a murmur of anticipation rippled through the room; the "expectant crowd was not disappointed," the paper reported. Jailer Hening brought back with him, for his first appearance in court, Charles Watkins, newly indicted for the murder of his wife. He walked in with "a most dramatic attitude."

Watkins had always been a dapper dresser, and somehow, he was able to continue this affectation even in jail. He wore, the *Roanoke Times* reported, a black suit, a white shirt with a standing collar and a checkered vest. In the buttonhole of his lapel was a spray of pink geraniums, although who gave him these was left unsaid. "Every eye in the courtroom was focused on him," the paper recounted, and he "looked as if he felt conspicuous. He coughed uneasily several times and was frequently arranging part of his dress."

Yet the most surprising aspect of his appearance was scarcely noted by the reporter: he came before Judge Griffin's bench alone. He had no attorney to represent him in a trial for his life.

Why this would be is almost incomprehensible. But it perhaps indicates again that Charles was in a state of denial, not appreciating the severity of his situation. Earlier in the week he had indicated to the *Roanoke Times* reporter his desire to employ Colonel George Hansbrough and A.B. Pugh as his attorneys and seems to have met with them at least once. When asked by the incredulous judge about the absence of any legal counsel, Watkins stated that these two prominent attorneys would represent him. But neither was in the courtroom for his arraignment, neither had been actually retained for the case, and it appears neither was even aware of his appearance in court. Charles Watkins stood before the bench with only imaginary lawyers.

Quickly Judge Griffin sent for Hansbrough, who was obviously nearby. The respected attorney, who had months earlier secured Ida Friebel's release from custody, rushed into the courtroom, no doubt a bit confused why. After hearing an explanation, Hansbrough said that he had not been employed by the defendant but would serve for the moment as Watkins's representation, if there could be a continuance. Charles, for his part, quickly agreed: he was not ready for trial, "on account of the absence of his witnesses."

Judge Griffin, no doubt annoyed at this important trial beginning with such disarray, could only agree. He ordered the case be continued until the next session of county court in August—only a couple of weeks away.

Charles Watkins was led up the aisle and back to the jail, with the eyes of his former neighbors watching him in silence.

FOR REASONS NEVER EXPLAINED, but most likely simply because of a lack of available time, Colonel Hansbrough would have no further involvement with the Watkins case. Instead, Arthur Benton Pugh would take over the case as lead counsel for Watkins's defense. In addition, his associates William W. Moffett and Marshall Gwin McClung would assist him. To borrow the phrase from a much later highly publicized murder trial, these three comprised a "dream team" of lawyers to try to keep the noose from around Charles's neck.

Arthur B. Pugh was born in 1854 in Hampshire County, Virginia, one of the counties that would form West Virginia in his early childhood as a result of the Civil War. Beginning life working on the family farm, Pugh showed enough promise and gumption in the postwar years to get the opportunity for an education at the University of Virginia. He studied law and was admitted to the West Virginia bar in 1876. He worked for several lucrative practices before accepting a position with the federal government in Washington, D.C., assisting primarily with land cases related to the expansion of the all-important railroads stitching the American countryside.

But "not finding official life at Washington entirely suited to his tastes," Pugh relocated to the quieter life but promising business environment of the Roanoke Valley. In 1890, he settled at Salem, rather than the frenzied metropolis of Roanoke, and opened a legal office. In the few months since he had moved to Salem, he had rapidly achieved a reputation for legal talent. His future in Salem looked bright.[25]

Pugh's associate William Walter Moffett was a native of Culpeper County, Virginia, born in 1854 into a respected and long-pedigreed family. As a young man, he "read law" in the firm of an uncle in Rappahannock County, passing the bar in 1877. However, rather than practice the legal profession at first, he became editor of a newspaper and in 1883 was elected to the state legislature. Following his term in Richmond, Moffett relocated to Washington, D.C., and finally started a lucrative legal career. But only a few months before the Watkins trial, he had moved to Salem and hung his shingle.[26]

Although none of the biographical information about Pugh and Moffett explains the professional relationship between the two, the fact that both attorneys came from Washington, D.C., to Salem in the same year was likely more than coincidence. It's certainly in the realm of possibility that the pair met in the nation's capital, developed a rapport and agreed to relocate to the quieter town of Salem and join forces in a legal collaboration. Salem, a county seat next to the boisterous railroad town of Roanoke, was an ideal place to make a new start.

The junior member of the defense team was Marshall Gwin McClung, only twenty-seven and as yet unmarried. Born in West Virginia in 1864, he was only beginning his legal career, but by the end of his life (1932) he would be respected enough to have the words "a lawyer of ability and integrity" engraved on his tombstone.

It is unclear how, or if, this dream team was ever to be paid for their efforts. Watkins had little money and, despite his claims to the contrary, seemed to have no friends to subsidize his legal fees. While the Sixth Amendment guaranteed the accused representation, it would only be in the twentieth century that the associated expenses would be routinely borne by the taxpayer. It is not impossible that the defense attorneys were paid with public funds, but no clear evidence of this survives. So it may also be that they took on the task at their own expense.

Why would they do so, given that almost anyone looking at the evidence would conclude that Watkins had little chance of an acquittal? Perhaps they believed it simply to be the right thing to do. Charles Watkins was on trial for his life. He needed representation. Even assuming all the evidence pointed to his guilt, he had to receive the presumption of innocence, had to have the right to make his case before a jury. And even if (as seems likely from contemporary press accounts) a large majority of the Roanoke Valley's population wanted him to hang, procedure had to be followed. Such a high-profile case had to be handled properly, with no hint of mismanagement.

For Pugh, Moffett and McClung, it was also not necessarily a bad career move to take on Watkins's defense. All were fairly new to the bar in the area, and a case of this notoriety, even if a losing effort, would inevitably bring them attention and earn them respect. The summer after the trial, Pugh and Moffett would serve in another high-profile case, this time as the prosecution for an arson charge. (Private attorneys were often employed in this capacity in nineteenth-century Virginia.) The *Roanoke Times* noted on August 20, 1982, that "Pugh and Moffett were the lawyers who made such a determined defense of Watkins, and [the defendant] has much to fear with lawyer Pugh as prosecutor."

They may not save Watkins from the scaffold, but in the effort, reputations would be built. None of the three defense attorneys necessarily wanted to be forever branded as the man who tried to set a wife-murderer free. But to be known as good lawyers who could handle a challenging case with eloquence and competence, giving an accused man a spirited defense—this was not such a bad thing. If Charles Watkins's story was to end on the gallows, it would not be because three capable attorneys hadn't done their best to prevent it.

FOR THE PROSECUTION, COMMONWEALTH'S Attorney William Wirt Ballard would make the case against Watkins.

A Maryland native of fifty-six years, Ballard was among the minority of Marylanders who had supported the Confederacy in the Civil War. His military record as an officer was impressive and extensive, but poor health led to his leaving the service in the winter of 1863. He recuperated for the winter in Craig County, Virginia, apparently developing an attachment to the place before reentering the Confederate army—oddly, as a private—for the last months of the war, surrendering with Lee at Appomattox.

Prosecutor William W. Ballard. *Roanoke County Libraries.*

Afterward, Ballard returned to a study of the law that had been interrupted by the war. He moved to Craig County and was admitted to the bar, serving soon after as Commonwealth's Attorney for the sparsely populated county north of Roanoke. In 1868, he was offered a position as a professor of classical languages at an upstart school known as Preston and Olin College in Blacksburg, Virginia—an institution later to be known as Virginia Tech. In 1871, he relocated to Salem and reentered the legal profession, also serving as superintendent of schools for Roanoke County. Widely respected and locally influential, he was elected to the position of Commonwealth's Attorney for Roanoke County in 1891—just in time to take over the prosecution of Charles Watkins.[27]

And so the lines were drawn. A room full of educated, respected, professional legal experts would battle over the fate of one Charles H. Watkins, accused wife murderer. Each man had a job to do and an obligation to do it well. They would make arguments and objections, interrogate witnesses and try to impugn testimony, punch and counterpunch—not with fists, but with legal terminology and technical jargon and occasional sly humor. When the proceedings were gaveled closed, they would go on to other cases, sometimes as allies, sometimes opponents. Outside of the courtroom, they would sit on committees together, worship in the same churches, attend the same social functions, go to the weddings of one another's daughters, members of a close-knit confederacy of friends. Moffett and Ballard were members of the same Masonic lodge in Salem, as was the presiding judge.

But for now, they were on opposite sides of the aisle, and one side would win, while the other would lose. It was how the game was played. They were friends and colleagues but obliged for the moment to stand on opposite fields of battle, each eager to give their own answer to a most important question: did Charles Watkins murder his wife Susan in cold blood?

PRESIDING OVER THE COURTROOM was Judge Wingfield Griffin. Born in 1846, Griffin came from a prosperous and influential family in Salem. The illustrious brothers of his family—the Fighting Griffins they were dubbed—had mostly served with distinction in the Civil War. Charles had commanded an artillery unit up through Appomattox, where his unit (the Salem Flying Artillery, in which George Zirkle had served) claimed the distinction of firing the last cannon of Lee's Army of Northern Virginia. John had served as a chaplain in the war; Samuel had been a cavalry major. A younger brother, Thomas, was not old enough to serve in the Civil War, but he enlisted in the navy afterward and in his long, distinguished career would serve in the Spanish-American War and retire as a commodore.

As for Wingfield, he also was too young to serve his beloved Confederacy with his brothers, so he enrolled at the Virginia Military Institute. But when the desperation of the South led to the enlistment of ever younger (and older) soldiers, teenage Wingfield left school and hurriedly signed on with a "cradle and grave" unit. He saw little action but proudly wore the gray.

After the war, he studied law and, in 1874, was appointed to the Roanoke County Court (only a year after passing the bar).[28] Judge Griffin was widely respected for his judicial temperament and community leadership. He would preside over this trial with no-nonsense equanimity and an unshakable commitment to proper legal procedure.

Wingfield Griffin, in his U.S. Volunteer uniform from the Spanish-American War. *Salem Historical Society.*

ON SUNDAY, AUGUST 16, the *Roanoke Times* reported that Watkins's trial might be heard at the August session of court, although at this point which courtroom—the circuit or the county court—was still not known. The answer was revealed the next day when Watkins was led before the bench of Roanoke County Court and Judge Griffin. But the paper's assumption that the trial would commence was premature.

With Watkins ("dandily dressed and apparently rather nervous") watching silently from the defendant's seat, his attorneys Arthur Pugh and William Moffett moved immediately for a continuance. Pugh told the judge that he had only been employed on the case the following Thursday, and although he had "spent Friday, Saturday, and, he regretted to say, part of Sunday on the case," he was simply not ready to proceed.

Prosecutor Ballard was given the opportunity to express his opinion on the matter, and not surprisingly, he opposed the continuance. "A lawyer [is] always supposed to be ready!" teased Ballard, in what appears to be the first of several instances of good-natured jibing between the defense and prosecution. I've "never heard of a continuance being granted because a lawyer wanted to look over his law books," Ballard mocked.

"I never made any such statement," countered Pugh, taking (probably mock) offense at the hint that he did not know his craft. Little of the dialogue is preserved in the newspaper accounts, but the discussion then seemed to center on the question of witnesses—Pugh could not proceed with the defense of the accused until an unnamed witness or witnesses were available. Ballard, ever the cagey prosecutor, tried to squeeze some information out of his opponent, the better to prepare his own case. "Have you a witness?" "I don't propose to discourse" on that subject, responded Pugh.

Perhaps hidden in that brief exchange was one of the questions overshadowing the Watkins case: did anyone know the whereabouts of Ida Friebel? She would certainly be able to give testimony of interest to both defense and prosecution. But that issue remained a mystery.

Griffin made a quick decision, and the only one, in fairness, he could. Watkins was on trial for his life, and the attorneys representing him were unprepared to proceed on this day. He ordered the case continued until the September session of his court. The accused wife murderer was led back to his cell in the jail behind the courthouse, and the court turned its attention to other matters.

Twelve days later, on August 29, the *Roanoke Times* reporter, under the "Salem News" column, gave an update on Watkins's status. "Confinement is beginning to tell upon Charles Watkins, colored, who is incarcerated in the County jail at Salem, awaiting trial," began the story, seemingly based on a visit by the reporter. "The shadow of the gallows is enveloping slowly, but surely."

For the first time, the recipient of Charles's "fatal letter" was revealed in press accounts to be Benjamin Wright. But that fact was mentioned only in passing, not as a shocking exposé. This would suggest that Ben Wright's role in the location and arrest of his cousin was already public knowledge, the subject, no doubt, of extensive local gossip. The letter is described as a "confession that [Watkins] killed his wife." The writer opines that the testimony of Wright and Taylor Watkins will be damning, though noting that "how much truth there is in [such rumors] no one but the authorities know and they will not talk."

THE SEPTEMBER TERM OF county court convened on the twenty-third. More than a month had passed, weeks in which Pugh and his team no doubt spent considering their defense. We can surmise what they had discovered: the evidence did not look good for their client. If they interviewed people familiar with the case—Taylor and Lucy Watkins, the Wrights, the Washingtons—they certainly would have found little evidence that pointed to Charles's innocence. It does not appear that they had access to the letter to Ben Wright, however.

Only a few factors played in their favor. Much of the evidence they could count on Ballard presenting was entirely circumstantial. No one had witnessed the actual murder. No murder weapon had been found. Witnesses could place Charles and Susan in the same place the morning of the murder, but she was alive the last anyone saw her. If this sliver of hope could be utilized to raise doubt even in one jury member, perhaps Pugh could win his hopeless case. Perhaps.

Another hope—a fleeting, improbable one—would be if a witness could be found. In the best-case scenario, someone would be willing to testify that they saw Charles miles away from the scene of the crime at the time of the murder. But, like most best-case scenarios, this was a far-fetched hope.

Still, witnesses for the defense would be useful—character witnesses for Charles, perhaps, or someone willing to paint Susan as a difficult wife, less of a victim. Did such witnesses exist? From Pugh's perspective, only time would tell. He hadn't found them yet.

On Monday, September 21, the case of Charles Watkins was on the docket for Judge Griffin's court. And once again, not surprisingly, the defense moved for a continuance. Pugh needed the continuance because, as reported the *Roanoke Times* on the twenty-third, that he "desired the presence of witnesses from Milwaukee and Chicago."

At the same hearing, some fifteen witnesses ("mostly colored," noted the *Times*) were recognized to appear at the next session of the court for the prosecution. But who were the witnesses from Milwaukee and Chicago that Pugh hoped to bring to Virginia to testify? No names are given, but one was almost certainly on Pugh's wish list.

Pugh was trying to find Edith "Ida" Friebel.

And why not? Her testimony would certainly have bearing on the case. It stands to reason that Ballard would have been eager to depose her as well, though not as urgently. Ballard didn't need Friebel to make his case of Watkins's guilt.

But Pugh might conceivably find her a key witness.

There might be a chance—a remote chance, even a fool's chance—that a claim of self-defense might keep the noose from Charles's neck. On August 29, the *Roanoke Times* had speculated that this might be a likely defense strategy. Referring to the Ben Wright letter, as then publicly unseen but with some contents leaked, the paper surmised that "the excuse that he did it because he was afraid she would kill him will hardly be accepted as true."

But how could the defense introduce testimony to this effect? No eyewitnesses could be found in Virginia who could say that Susan had ever threatened her husband—indeed, there's no real reason to think that she ever did. Still, perhaps one or more such witnesses, perhaps friends of Charles who would take his side, were among those Pugh wanted to call from out of state. Note that he used the plural: "desired the presence of *witnesses* from Milwaukee and Chicago" [emphasis added].

Charles might make a self-defense case for himself, and indeed he did informally at times. On the night before the murder, he had told his uncle Taylor that Susan had threatened him; the letter to Ben Wright made a similar claim. Charles could certainly say this under oath. But Pugh was far too savvy an attorney to put his unpredictable client on the stand, subject to Ballard's cross-examination. That left only one human anywhere who might be able to speak to any trouble in the marriage of Susan and Charles Watkins: his lover, Ida Friebel.

No documentary evidence survives of any search for Ida, of any subpoena that might have been issued, of any requests for information that might have been sent to officials in Chicago or Milwaukee. But it's reasonable to assume that such existed in the late summer of 1891 and were sufficiently crucial to the defense to request another delay in the proceedings.

Judge Wingfield Griffin ordered the continuance, vocally expressing regret about the delay. Pugh got down to business, making the most of his month's reprieve. But in the end, Edith Friebel was not to be located and had no reason to want to be found.

THE NEXT DAY, COUNTY court was able to dispose of some of the business related to the case. Judge Griffin was asked by Commonwealth's Attorney Ballard to assign someone to take care of the "goods and chattels" of the estate of Susan Watkins, which as far as they knew consisted of the two steamer trunks she had left at the Roanoke depot the day she arrived. Sheriff Zirkle would administer the estate, and F.C. Burdett, W.L. Brand, B.G. Morgan, Millard Huff and Watts Dillard were appointed commissioners for appraising the items and organizing a public auction to offset the county expenditures on the case. Dillard, it may be recalled, was the pharmacist/physician whom Charles and Susan were supposedly traveling to see the morning she was murdered. Huff would double as the auctioneer.

The auction was held on the courthouse steps in Salem on October 19, as briefly described in a previous chapter. Both of the local papers reported on the proceedings, describing a crowd of bidders both black and white. The most expensive item was a pair of diamond earrings, purchased by one J.W. McDonald for $46.25. Auctioneer Huff himself procured a gold watch for $22.25. Other items of jewelry went for lesser amounts, as low a nickel for a single breast pin, generally purchased by white bidders. Several African American bidders took an interest in Susan's clothes, which were high quality. Among the bidders was George Washington, who purchased a velvet perfume holder for his wife. But Ben Wright proved to be one of the most active bidders, probably more for practicality than sentiment. He bid on a number of pieces of Susan's clothing at a good price, presumably for his wife and daughters. He got a silk dress for $3.75, two beaded capes for a total of $3.00, a pair of shoes for $1.75 and various other small items. Finally, he bid $5.15 for one of the trunks to carry it all home.

In the end, Susan's goods and chattels, all that she had left behind besides whispers of tragedy, fetched a total amount of $151.40.

On September 25, after county court had adjourned for the month, the *Roanoke Times* lamented the lack of closure in the Watkins case and gave a reading of prevailing public opinion. "Considerable indignation has been expressed at the continued postponement of the Watkins trial," the paper opined, presumably accurately. "Conservative citizens don't like to see the state put so much expense in endeavoring to save the neck of one who so richly deserved hanging."

And yet at the October court, another continuance was requested and granted, and for the same reason: "on the grounds of witnesses being absent," reported the *Times* on October 20.

In all of the press coverage of the Watkins affair, there is never any direct reference to the rights of the accused. And yet this concept permeated every procedure of the court. Charles Watkins lived in a day when the color of his skin decided how he would be treated in the larger society; yet in Griffin's courtroom he was granted the presumption of innocence, the right to representation, the right to make his case and, through his attorneys, the right to seek continuances for legitimate reasons. Judge Griffin seemed to bristle at the delay stretching from July through November over a crime committed in April, at one point calling it all "a mighty slow process." The wheels of justice normally moved more quickly in those days.

Yet Griffin granted three consecutive continuances to the defense, because the rights of the accused demanded them. Public opinion may have believed Charles Watkins "richly deserved hanging." But it would not happen without a trial that was properly administered. One needn't look far into the history of crime and punishment in the South of Jim Crow to find the rights of accused minorities being trampled. But that was not the case in this particular trial.

But that being said, there were limits to the indulgence of the court. Arthur Pugh could have his continuances to seek witnesses, but they would not last forever. Griffin was willing to make allowances for the defense, but his indulgence was not unlimited. Eventually, the fate of Charles Watkins would be decided as the "mighty slow process" moved to a conclusion.

While Watkins spent his months in a cell awaiting trial, other crimes in southwest Virginia attracted public attention and provide interesting comparisons to the case at hand.

On August 15, two Italian immigrants, a stonemason named C. Mosca and his friend Vittorio Tomat, were walking home late at night to their boardinghouse in Buchanan, Virginia, on the James River in nearby Botetourt County. Two other men passed them on the dark road, then abruptly turned on them and pulled guns, demanding their valuables. While one man searched Tomat for money, the other held the guns. Mosca jumped and grappled with the gunman. A shot rang out, and Mosca fell, dying a short while later.

The two assailants, both black, fled, and the next day a manhunt ensued. As happened in the Watkins case, there were cases of mistaken identity, as two men were arrested in Salem but released when they could provide unimpeachable alibis.

By September 8, however, all of the evidence in Mosca's murder was pointing to a nineteen-year-old from Salem named Henry Nowlin, alias Henry Law, alias "Batting Henry." He had a criminal record, having been convicted of housebreaking the year before. A William McCarthy was initially believed to be his accomplice in the murder.

Soon word reached investigators that Nowlin had been arrested in Wytheville and transferred to Lynchburg (although if in connection to the Mosca case or for another charge is not entirely clear). Tomat was brought to the jail to see him and readily identified Nowlin as the gunman.

Nowlin made little effort at that point to conceal his crime and willingly identified his accomplice not as McCarthy, but a known troublemaker named Will Dandridge, also from Salem. The two men had attended some sort of festival at a church in Buchanan in August and were walking home to Salem (a distance of some thirty miles). When they passed the two men, they spontaneously decided to rob them. Nowlin claimed reluctance, offering instead to give Dandridge half of the five dollars he had with him, but the latter refused and insisted the two hapless pedestrians had money for the taking. Dandridge was armed but gave his pistols to Nowlin, leading to the tragic turn of events.

Nowlin was tried for murder at the Botetourt County Courthouse in Fincastle on September 25. As he had confessed, the trial took little time. Nowlin was sentenced to death and was hanged on November 20 (coincidentally the day a verdict was announced in the Watkins trial). In jail, Nowlin made a profession of religion and gave a full and eloquent confession to the press, as was almost obligatory for condemned men in those days.

Dandridge, however, had fled immediately after the crime, and, as Charles Watkins had attempted, succeeded in melting into anonymity somewhere. He was never apprehended and never answered for his part in the crime, at least on this side of eternity.

There was a rather disturbing epilogue to the Nowlin case. Henry Hale, Nowlin's stepfather, sent two hired men to Fincastle mere hours after the hanging to return his stepson's remains to Salem. The sheriff there was not expecting any family to claim the body and had already placed it in a whiskey barrel to ship to a university in West Virginia. Medical schools in those days frequently claimed the bodies of executed criminals for use as cadavers. Hale's couriers, however, protested vociferously and understandably, and Nowlin's remains were released to them. He was laid to rest the next day in Salem, next to a sister who had predeceased him. The burial was presumably in East Hill North, the same "colored" cemetery where Susan Watkins was at rest.

Nowlin's trial occurred five weeks after the crime and two weeks after he was arrested; he was executed less than two months after that. The entire affair—from crime to hanging—fits into only a portion of Watkins's time in jail. While modern observers might find in this level of speed a rush to judgment, it was customary in the 1890s. It's little wonder Judge Griffin deemed the Watkins case "a mighty slow process."

ANOTHER HOMICIDE THAT BRIEFLY stirred gossip in Salem was the Circus Murder of 1891. In September, Rentz Circus, described by the *Roanoke Times* as a "slim affair with only one little elephant," arrived in Salem under the management of one Mr. DeArly. While circuses, even slim ones, were popular entertainment for small towns, the performers were often considered a menace by locals and certainly not fit for polite company.

On the evening of September 24 or the following morning, Buck Toner, a "jack tar" and performer on the tightrope and trapeze, got into an argument at a hotel bar with fellow performer Harry Evans (or Evantine), described as the "lecturer" for the circus—more or less what we today would call the emcee. The two men took their quarrel outside of the Revere Hotel where the troupe was staying, and Toner struck Evans with a bottle or other implement hard enough to fracture the skull.

Toner immediately fled, and Evans was taken into the hotel, unconscious. Local physicians arrived but could do little to relieve the growing pressure on Evans's brain; the unfortunate performer lingered until October 2, when he died with his devoted wife at his bedside.

Sheriff George Zirkle was already on the trail of Toner even before the case became a homicide. But he had little luck. Although he followed the Rentz Circus up the railroad tracks as far as Abingdon, no one seemed to know anything about Toner's whereabouts. (Circus people were notorious for covering the tracks of other circus people.) Once again, Zirkle's search was hampered by the absence of a suitable reward and by the lack of funding for pursuing fugitives. Eventually, the trail grew even colder and Zirkle had to concede that this fugitive was likely to get away with murder.

Indeed, Buck Toner was never put on trial for the crime. But two years later, on August 13, 1893, he slipped while performing a trapeze act in Erie, Pennsylvania. Toner was killed by the fall.

A FINAL INCIDENT OCCURRED in October in the small town of Clifton Forge in Alleghany County, Virginia. On October 17, a band of eight rowdy and drunken miners, all African American, came to Clifton Forge from the nearby community of Iron Gate. Their unruly behavior soon attracted the attention of the local police, but when an attempt was made to arrest them, several white onlookers stepped into the fray. A riot ensued in the sleepy little town. Four of the gang were wounded and arrested; the police dutifully took them to jail.

However, the angry white mob was not about to lose its prey. They broke into the jail and dragged the four inmates into the street. One man made an impassioned plea for the youngest of the four (only sixteen), and the teenager was released by the mob. But the other three were lynched, in yet another episode of the ugliness which could mar justice in the South.

The Clifton Forge lynchings demonstrated that the justice system in small Virginia towns could often move in much more violent directions than it did in the Charles Watkins case.

8

"WILL HE OR THE JURY HANG?"

The proceedings were interesting, that was certain. At least in their newness to J.H. Pedigo. He didn't get to the county seat very often and had never been in a courtroom before. So the novelty of the thing caught his attention; the established routine, the mild pageantry, the seriousness of it all. Still, on the whole he'd prefer to be back in Vinton and uninvolved in any way. But then, he didn't think he'd spend much time here once he said what he was compelled to say.

Jury duty, he knew, was the obligation of a citizen, and all things being equal he would be happy to serve. But not this case. The violence of it all gave him a sinking feeling in the pit of his stomach. Pedigo was a gentle man and a quiet one, and he couldn't imagine a husband committing violence against his wife. Glancing at the defendant sitting placidly across the room, he wondered if it was true, or how it could be true. The man didn't look like a killer.

The day was dragging on. When the court had convened at 10:00 a.m., both the prosecution and the defense were perturbed by the absence of one witness, a cousin of the accused. The judge was clearly annoyed. But he adjourned the court and vowed to go himself to find the errant witness. Pedigo and the rest of the jury pool were escorted back to the hotel, where they whiled away the time reading, playing checkers, napping.

Now, after a midday meal, court was back in session. Some preliminary business was dispensed, and it was time to start selecting men for the jury. Since the case was so well known in Salem, the court had sent for the venire (jury pool) from Vinton, clear across the county. Of course, folks in Vinton read the papers too, and Pedigo had heard the gossip for months. He looked around at the other fifteen men, his neighbors, most of whom Pedigo knew well.

Although Pedigo had never been through the process, he understood how it would work. The prosecutor would ask each man some questions, trying to determine his suitability to serve. The main one would be along the lines of "is there any reason you should not be named a juror?

One by one the Vintonians were queried. Most were willing to serve and were easily selected. But not all. Old Mr. Kasey begged to be excused on account of his age, and neither prosecutor nor defense had an objection. Mr. Thrasher and Mr. Preston, two leading citizens, confessed that they had formed an opinion as to the guilt of the defendant. The defense attorney Pugh was all too happy to excuse them.

At last, Mr. Ballard stood came to his seat. "Mr. Pedigo, how are you?"

"I am well, sir, and hope you are the same."

"Tell me, Mr. Pedigo, are you familiar with the case before the court today?"

"I have some vague familiarity about it from the newspapers, but I can't say that I've formed any opinion about it."

"Good, good. So tell me, is there any reason you should be excused as juror?"

Pedigo shifted slightly in his seat and cleared his throat. "Mr. Ballard, Your Honor, I can't say if that man is or is not guilty of killing his wife. But this I do know. I cannot in any way countenance the death penalty. Even if he's guilty, he is still a child of God. If I am asked to serve, I will not in good conscience be able to vote to send him to the gallows."

A murmur ran through the packed courtroom. Pedigo knew his convictions were a minority opinion, but he would not contradict them merely to serve on a jury. He sensed more than saw some of the others in the jury box shake their heads in amazement. But Mr. Ballard did not seem particularly dismayed, beyond a slightly cocked eyebrow at the curiosity of it. "Your Honor, in light of the fact that this is a capital crime, I suggest we dismiss this juror."

Judge Griffin looked over at the defense table. Mr. Pugh shrugged. The judge spoke: "Mr. Pedigo, you are dismissed. Thank you for coming in today."

Pedigo arose, shook hands with the men to his right and left and strolled up the aisle. Perhaps he could catch Mr. Kasey and help him onto the streetcar for the hour-long ride home. He felt a few eyes follow him as he departed, but he walked out with a clear conscience. He glanced sideways at the defendant, still sitting as if detached from the proceedings. Pedigo had the sudden thought that he was looking at a man already dead. He had no illusions as to the likely end of the case—a hood, a rope, a lever. Many would call it justice, and he could—to a point—understand their perspective. But he could not share that opinion.

But J.H. Pedigo was relieved that he would have to play no part in the tragic drama to come.

J.H. HENING AWOKE WITH a start. The jailhouse cook was shaking him, saying something about an escape upstairs. Hening sat bolt upright, panic stabbing at his stomach. Throwing some clothes on and grabbing his revolver, he ran to investigate. His first thought was certainly for the most desperate criminals, held in ground-floor cells of the overcrowded jail. Quickly he ascertained that no cells were empty.

Hening breathed a sigh of relief. Charles Watkins, the most notorious inmate in the Roanoke County jail, was still securely in his cell, asleep.

It was November 6, 1891, and Hening had only been on the job as deputy sheriff and jailer since July. He must have known that there would be hell to pay for any escape, but if Watkins, a man who had eluded capture for months, had gone missing, it would likely mean his job. Although he could (and probably did) argue that he was not at fault. The county jail was far from secure. Bars were on windows and cell entryways but not through the simple brick walls.

Content that nothing was amiss on the ground floor, Hening proceeded upstairs to the other cells. In the upper cell in the northwest corner, he found a gaping hole knocked through the brick wall. Five prisoners were missing. Two others who had only short sentences remaining had stayed in their cells, claiming, perhaps implausibly, that they had heard nothing.

Missing were John Massie and William Broomfield, both wanted for theft, a moonshiner named Sam Adams, a Radford criminal being held in Salem named Don Cook and a John Rogers, described as a "one-armed Negro," who was imprisoned on a morals charge. The *Roanoke Times* report the next morning on the jail break surmised that the prisoners had slowly picked the mortar out from between the three courses of brick, concealing their work with a blanket. They waited until the night of the escape to knock out the outside course, which would have been noticeable outside. Once through the wall, they knotted their blankets together and climbed down to the yard (although how the man with one arm accomplished this is not explained). By the time Hening got to the upper cells, they had vanished into the night.[29]

Watkins, however, was still in custody, having played no part in the escape. In time, Hening would come to look on Charles as a model prisoner. He behaved himself, kept himself and his cell clean and caused no trouble. The papers make mention of kindnesses expressed by the Hening family to Charles, and Charles would later speak of a Bible given to him by Mrs. Hening.

Surprisingly, in fact, on two occasions Charles came to the defense of his jailers. As reported in the *Roanoke Times* on December 22, 1891, Charles briefly shared a cell with three other prisoners who were being transported to the state penitentiary. These prisoners had smuggled in brickbats and secreted them in the stovepipe of the cell, intending to use them to attack Hening. Once he could safely do so out of sight of the other prisoners, Charles removed the bats and gave them to the deputy. The plot was averted.

On another occasion (Hening did not indicate exactly when in Watkins's five-month imprisonment these things happened), some prisoners from Roanoke City were temporarily housed in Salem, and they collected pieces of hard coal to use as weapons in an escape attempt. Charles surreptitiously passed a note to Hening, again saving the day.

Watkins had always been charming, outgoing and affable, and even in prison his personal magnetism was evident. But if Hening appreciated having him in one of his cells, it was not to last. The start of the long-delayed trial was finally at hand.

THE OPENING OF THE November session of the Roanoke County Court was scheduled for Monday, the sixteenth. Three times since his arrest, Charles Watkins had stood before Judge Griffin and claimed, through his attorneys, that the trial could not proceed. Absent witnesses were too detrimental to the defense case; the court had no alternative but to agree.

But if the patience of the court was long, it was not endless. At last, there would be no further continuances, no ongoing hunt for out-of-state witnesses. The trial would unquestionably commence this month, a fact that must have been made clear to Pugh by some means. Don't bother asking for another delay, he must have been told, or perhaps he simply assumed this instinctively. Pugh, accordingly, would not seek another continuance. He and his team would arrive at the courthouse ready to

The Roanoke County Courthouse about the time of the Watkins trial. *Salem Historical Society.*

defend their client, to offer any evidence, any testimony, any objection to the proceedings that might inspire that elusive reasonable doubt in the minds of at least one juror.

Judge Wingfield Griffin took his seat a few minutes before 10:00 a.m. on November 16, 1891. He expected promptness from everyone involved in his courtroom, and customarily, he set the example by arriving ahead of schedule. By the time the clocks chimed, all of the principal players were in place. Led in by jailer Hening, the defendant wore a dark suit and a new cravat, looking the part of the "dudish head-waiter," reported the *Roanoke Times.* Lawyers took their seats, prospective jurors and subpoenaed witnesses found their places, an eager crowd jockeyed for standing room in the packed-out courtroom. There was an undercurrent of anticipation in the courtroom, a murmur of voices waiting for the cry of "Order in the Court." It was time, after months of delay. The trial of the *Commonwealth of Virginia vs. Charles H. Watkins* was underway.[30]

Like his brother who would become a naval commodore, Griffin ran a tight ship. He made it clear often during the proceedings that he had little patience for delays—especially in a case he had planned to hear the previous August. But as soon as the proceedings were gaveled to order, a hitch arose.

A roll call of witnesses was held, and one key witness was absent. Addie Anderson was not in the courtroom.

The cousin of the defendant was described, interestingly, as an important witness for both the prosecution and the defense. An embarrassed Sheriff Zirkle stepped forward to explain. He, and a police sergeant named Wright from Roanoke City, had tried for days to locate Anderson and serve her a summons to appear, but to no avail. He said he had looked at the Hotel Felix, at a school called the Alleghany Institute and at the home of a railroad official named Mr. Cocke, all places Addie was known to work on occasion. They were certain she had recently been in the city, but no one had located her. Lawrence Anderson and Taylor and Lucy Watkins, her relatives, were all witnesses to be called and presumably, if not in the courtroom, were nearby. If so, they apparently could offer no clues as to her whereabouts.

Neither side was willing to proceed without her, and the very real prospect of another month's delay seemed a likely possibility. Griffin, to say the least, was highly annoyed.

Mulling for a moment, Griffin decided on another course of action. Rather than delay for a month, he would adjourn the court until 2:00 p.m. In the interim, Zirkle was ordered to proceed to Roanoke and find the wayward witness. And to be sure that the job was done properly, Griffin announced that he himself would go with the sheriff. Watkins was led back to his cell adjacent to the courthouse, and the jury panel was taken out to while away the next few hours.

Traveling to Roanoke and back meant nearly an hour and a half on the streetcar, leaving the men a little over two hours to find Addie in the teeming city. Yet they did so. Exactly how the judge and the sheriff knew where to look on such short notice was never explained, but indeed they located Addie Anderson at the home of Mr. Cocke, where Zirkle had failed to find her before. It is unclear why the earlier efforts had proven fruitless, but it may be that Addie, knowing she would be subpoenaed, had hidden out somewhere to avoid the courtroom and the necessity of testifying against her cousin. Or for him—both Ballard and Pugh had her on their list of witnesses.

If such was the case, when the sheriff and the presiding judge knocked at the door and told her to get her coat and immediately follow them, she certainly complied.

With everyone on the witness list accounted for, court reconvened promptly at 2:00 p.m. The first order of business was to bring formal charges against the defendant. Charles Watkins was presented with four separate but very similar counts. The first charge, as the *Roanoke Times* reported, was "having,

Two of the streetcars (or dummies) that ran between Roanoke City and Salem. *Salem Historical Society.*

on the 7th of April, murdered Susan J. Watkins by striking her on the head with a stick or wooden club." The three subsequent charges merely changed the suspected instrument of death: a stone or rock, a pistol and (as a final catch-all) some other "means unknown."

With the murder weapon unknown and never recovered, the prosecutor was hedging his bets against any technicality. But all four charges amounted to the same thing: first-degree murder.

As the charges were read, Pugh made a demurrer (objection) to each in turn—an expected but a futile strategy, as Griffin overruled him immediately each time. Like the good attorney he was, Pugh was seemingly trying to plant seeds of doubt in the mind of the jurors—this whole case is nonsense; pay no attention to what the prosecutor claims.

Now Watkins stood and was asked how he desired to plead. "Not guilty," he replied, to the surprise of no one.

Save whispered exchanges with his attorneys, these were the only two words he would speak in court until the jury pronounced a verdict.

NEXT ON THE DOCKET was the necessity of seating a jury. A venire of sixteen men had been selected from Vinton, a smaller but prosperous town at the other end of Roanoke County, whose citizens would presumably be less prejudicial toward the accused. As recounted in the chapter introduction, four men were dismissed—George Kasey on account of his age, S.F. Thrasher and N. Preston because they confessed that they were predisposed to assume Watkins's guilt and J.H. Pedigo because his opposition to the death penalty disqualified him from a capital case.

There remained then twelve men, "well-dressed and intelligent looking" as the paper described them, to decide the fate of Charles Watkins: John Jones, J.R. Richardson, Frank Gish, R.O. Smith, T.J. Burnett, Isaac Kelly, Jacob Vinyard, R.H. Rhodes, S.M. Muse, Joel Ridgeway, Griffin Lloyd and R.W. Bryant. These men were sworn as jurors and would be scrupulously sequestered at a nearby hotel for the duration of the trial.

AT LAST, IT WAS time to hear testimony. The witnesses for the prosecution were all sworn. Curiously, Addie Anderson was not one of them. Ballard, having insisted that morning that he required her testimony, seemingly had now decided not to call her. She would appear as a defense witness days later.

The first witness called by the prosecution was Lawrence Anderson, the young man who had first discovered Susan Watkins's remains seven months before. (Technically, a neighborhood boy named George Law had alerted Lawrence to the body in the creek, but George was too young to testify.)

Lawrence gave clear, coherent testimony about his recollections of that unforgettable day, describing, for instance, the position of the body in the creek. However, he admitted that he didn't take time to examine the corpse in exhaustive detail. "I didn't stay no longer than I could get in my wagon and go home. I was scared, and went home and told my mother," he confessed.

Pugh cross-examined the witness only slightly. Anderson had, after all, only described events that were not in question and did not necessarily implicate Charles Watkins. A body had been found in the creek—this was beyond dispute.

The next witness called was John Banks. Banks had viewed Susan's body while it was still in the creek, had stood guard over it that first night and was intimately familiar with the neighborhood. More damaging to the defense, however, was his testimony that he had passed Charles and Edith Friebel leaving the Gum Spring neighborhood on the way to Salem. This testimony therefore clearly placed Watkins in the vicinity of the crime. Banks also testified about footprints he observed at the scene of the murder: a woman's shoe with plated heels and a man's new overshoe, moving away from the scene.

Not surprisingly, Pugh spent more time cross-examining Banks—in fact, badgering him, the newspaper reporter claimed. None of the questions he asked survive, but they seemed to have revolved around the details of the scene—the distance to nearby landmarks, especially. Pugh asked questions in a way that may have confused a less confident witness, perhaps hoping to cause the jury to distrust the testimony before them. However, Banks rose to the occasion, sticking to his story. By the time he stood down at 4:30 p.m., the prosecution's case had been considerably bolstered.

4:30 seemed like a good quitting time to some. But Judge Griffin announced that he was determined to continue until at least 6:00 p.m., even if it meant lighting the gas lamps in the courtroom. However, Commonwealth's Attorney Ballard suddenly asked for adjournment, due to

The building in the center, with the balconies overlooking the street, is the Hotel Lucerne (later called the Crawford). The jury was housed here during the trial. *Salem Historical Society.*

a miserable headache that had begun to afflict him. The request "seemed to nettle the judge a little," the paper reported. But Ballard insisted he could not continue: "I'm downright sick!"

An annoyed Griffin relented. He reluctantly ordered the sheriff to take charge of the jury and sequester them for the night in the nearby Hotel Lucerne. With a sharp rap of his gavel, he declared the court adjourned.

Watkins began the by-now familiar walk back to his cell. Whether he slept soundly that night or stared into the darkness, wracked by anxiety, is not a detail preserved by history.

DAY TWO OF THE trial of Charles Watkins began, as the judge required, promptly at 10:00 a.m. All of the principal participants—attorneys, jury, the accused—were in their places, and a capacity crowd overfilled the public seats once again. As on the previous day, the bulk of the audience was African American.

Prosecutor Ballard, assumedly recovered from his headache, continued his case by calling Samuel Strickler to the stand, although he had not been named in the witness list the day before. Strickler had, with his neighbor John Banks, stood guard over Susan Watkins's remains that first night. He described in detail the position of the body when found, the clothing she was wearing and footprints on the bank. His testimony by and large agreed with Banks's of the previous afternoon.

Upon cross-examination, Pugh "tried hard to shake this witness," the *Roanoke Times* reported. But he did so on what must have seemed an arcane and insignificant point to the listeners: how secluded the scene of the murder was. Pugh tried to get Strickler to concede that the body in the stream could have been easily viewed by anyone passing on the adjacent path, but Strickler refused to agree to such a characterization of the scene.

Why did Pugh zero in on such trivial details of geography? His cross-examination tactics perhaps suggested a larger defense strategy. Perhaps Pugh was hoping to redraw the picture of the crime scene in the minds of the jury, to replace the sheltered "Dark Hollow" with a wide-open location next to a well-traveled thoroughfare. Perhaps the setting, so redefined, was a place where a body could not possibly have remained unseen for most of a day.

If the crime scene had been open and well trafficked, then perhaps the murder had occurred not early in the morning but mere minutes before Lawrence Anderson discovered the remains—hence long after Watkins and Ida had departed Gum Spring. Just maybe Charles was innocent, if the crime scene was so open to passersby. It was a remote chance, but perhaps, just perhaps, enough to raise a reasonable doubt in the mind of at least one juror.

But Strickler's testimony, unshaken by the questioning, gave Pugh no such opportunity to make that argument.

The next witness called was Charles Hatcher, another member of the coroner's jury (and a future sheriff of Roanoke County). Although months had passed since the murder, Hatcher had vivid memories of the crime scene to recount, even identifying the gold watch that was found under the body of Susan Watkins. Hatcher described the watch chain hanging from the left side of her body, while the watch was beneath her on the right side—suggesting someone had yanked the chain to retrieve the timepiece but had broken the chain in the attempt.

The prosecution now attempted a gimmick: Ballard produced for the jury a diagram of the Gum Spring neighborhood with the crime scene and nearby landmarks shown. The defense immediately objected—the sketch was not produced by a surveyor and hence could not be entirely accurate, Pugh complained. Judge Griffin sustained the objection and the map was discarded.

The cross-examination of Hatcher once again centered on the geography of the scene: "much time was consumed discussing the distances of different points in the neighborhood from the exact spot," the *Roanoke Times* summarized, without further explanation. Hatcher, however, maintained the same opinion of the matter as the previous witnesses: no one could easily see the body from the adjacent path, conceding only that a man on horseback might have been able to see over the foliage along the creek bed. Once again, Pugh's attempt to suggest the murder occurred in the wide open and probably after Charles had departed the neighborhood came to nothing. After this, Pugh did not revisit the question again.

The next two witnesses were Drs. Saunders and Baird, the presiding physicians from the coroner's inquest. Saunders took the stand first, describing the condition of the body and the wounds he had observed in his postmortem examination, conducted within twenty-four hours of death. Baird followed, his testimony mostly redundant to his colleague's, but added his opinion that death was instantaneous. Saunders especially made a fine witness for the prosecution, thought the *Roanoke Times* reporter on hand the next day, but Ballard made a tactical error. He asked Dr. Saunders what condition the body would have presented had Susan drowned, although the doctor had already noted that he did not examine her heart and lungs. The defense "made good use" of this error, although seemingly not with enough persuasion to undermine the testimony of two respected local physicians.

By the time Baird stepped down, it was 12:30 p.m., and Ballard suggested a lunch break. Griffin, ever the taskmaster, refused, and ordered another witness. George Washington was called to the stand and swore to tell the truth, the whole truth and nothing but the truth.

The *Roanoke Times*, hardly a bastion of racial sensitivity even for 1891, was rather dismissive of Washington in its coverage, calling him a "dark-skinned man…decidedly slow and hazy as a witness." Indeed, Washington's memory was confused on some important points, placing his last encounter with Charles Watkins in the fall of the year instead of the spring, and unable to recall Edith Friebel's full name. Nonetheless, his testimony got into the record important facts Ballard wanted the jury to consider about Susan's unexpected visit to his boardinghouse and about Charles's initial denial of being married to Susan. When Washington went on to describe a conversation he had with Susan (after confronting Charles in the street about the matter), the defense objected over the use of a dead woman's declaration as testimony.

While Judge Griffin considered the objection, the jury was taken out of the courtroom and a lengthy discussion was held. At last, the judge sustained Pugh's objection, and Washington's last statements were stricken from the record. It was but a small victory for the defense, but one quickly erased by the testimony of the next witnesses.

By this time, it was well past the noon hour, and Griffin relented in a brief recess. Upon returning after lunch, George Washington continued his testimony, most notably recounting that Charles, later on that tense day when he returned from the Hotel Felix, did concede that he was lawfully married to Susan. He also recounted details of the last time he'd seen Ida Friebel that Sunday and identified her from a photograph (exclaiming that Ida had given him an identical print).

On cross-examination, Pugh aggressively tried to undermine the credibility of George Washington. Before lunch, Washington had been unable to recall Edith's name; now he was her intimate friend exchanging cartes de visite. The implication, even the explication, was that during the recess someone had coached Washington and tainted his testimony. But Washington stuck to his story and denied any part of witness tampering.

Pugh's attempt got him nowhere. Had Washington been the only prosecution witness, perhaps the tactic might have worked. But others followed to corroborate his testimony, beginning with the next witness: his wife, Phyllis Washington.

Phyllis, having been (unlike her husband) at the boardinghouse when Ben Wright brought Susan to confront Charles, made an excellent eyewitness. She minutely detailed what had happened in her house the previous April and established that Susan had left with Charles the next day. She told of Ida's return for her trunk the following Wednesday, whereupon she was arrested. Perhaps most importantly, she testified that she had gone to Salem to see the body found in the creek and had identified her as the same Susan Wilson Watkins who had spent the night at her house.

"Cross examination failed to materially shake the evidence of Phyllis Washington," the *Roanoke Times* laconically reported. Pugh, no doubt, was beginning to feel the case slipping away from him.

Two subsequent witnesses helped to fill in the chronology of Susan's last day. J.C. Hathaway, a conductor for the streetcar, testified that he had seen Charles get on the dummy with a woman he did not know but described in detail. The two rode his car to the end of the line, as far west as they could go. Isaiah Reynolds, an acquaintance of Charles's, then testified that he had seen Charles with a woman in a black coat in Salem on the evening before the murder. Pugh had no questions for Hathaway; he only slightly cross-examined Reynolds. His defense was limping at best. The next witness would make things even worse.

Taylor Watkins was called to the stand.

THE UNCLE OF THE accused was a key witness for the prosecution. Ballard had, of course, done his homework and was counting on Taylor to introduce damning evidence not generally known by the public. It's not hard to imagine gasps from the gallery during his testimony.

In April, the Watkins family had instinctively circled their wagons around their wayward Charles: treating Susan as an unwelcome adversary, only cautiously telling their story to the authorities, failing to disclose key details voluntarily. They certainly did not condone murder and likely were the first people to be convinced of Charles's guilt. But, being members of an oppressed minority in a racist society, it was perhaps not their initial inclination to go out of their way in assisting the authorities against one of their own.

Seven months later, their instinct to protect Charles had evaporated. The shock of it all had faded; the idea that their relative had committed cold-blooded murder had hardened into inescapable fact. Taylor Watkins knew more about what transpired the night of the murder than anyone else on the witness list. And with resolution scrubbed of any pretense, he was ready to tell what had happened.

Taylor recounted how on April 6 Charles had arrived—alone—at the family's mountain cabin, ostensibly to see his ailing grandmother. But it was not long before he began lamenting the arrival of a woman claiming to be his wife, and, Charles claimed, threatening bodily harm against him and Ida. Taylor made a point of noting that Charles was wearing rubber overshoes.

The witness continued his story. As described in a previous chapter, it was not long before Charles saw Susan approaching the house, wounded and accusing her husband of shooting her. It is not clear how widely this detail—that Charles had become an attempted murderer before he ever arrived at his uncle's house—was generally known. The spectators must have reacted; perhaps Judge Griffin had to tap his gavel and call for order.

Taylor recounted the rest of the tense evening with little detail, but he asserted that Charles and Susan had left close to dawn, together. The defense team must have felt deflated. The testimony of the defendant's own uncle had given Charles motive, means and opportunity. The evidence pointed to an earlier, unsuccessful attempt at homicide. On cross-examination, Taylor never varied in the details of the story and, in fact, added another piece of the picture: that Ida was secreted in the cabin when Susan arrived.

Pugh hadn't lost the case yet. But realistic hopes for an acquittal had diminished enormously by the time Taylor Watkins stepped down.

Though the hour was growing late, there was still more testimony to hear. Fannie Coxe came to the stand next. If Ballard was trying to reconstruct a chronology of Charles's movements—from the Washingtons to the streetcar to Salem to Gum Spring—Coxe should have gone before Taylor Watkins. But she had not been in the courtroom earlier in the day; a messenger had to be dispatched to bring her to Salem. Now, if out of sequence, she added her part of the story—seeing Ida pass her home, followed later by Charles and a woman who was a stranger. Charles borrowed her lantern to get the woman across the log bridge. The next day, she testified, she'd seen Charles and Ida heading down the mountain, promising that Taylor would return the lantern later.

Finally, Lucy Watkins entered the witness box. Ballard decided to open by asking her about an elephant in the room: why her testimony to the coroner's inquest had been deceptively incomplete, omitting the relevant fact of Susan's nocturnal arrival at her home. Lucy answered that no one had asked her that question, so she had not answered it. Now, she would tell the whole truth, which differed little from her husband's testimony. She told of hearing pistol shots in the night before Charles arrived and added details that Taylor did not witness: how Charles came back to the cabin alone after leaving with Susan, how he and Ida left together later in the afternoon. From the prosecution standpoint, she was a solid witness—corroborating much of what had already been said under oath, adding more substance to the case against Charles Watkins.

The newspaper accounts do not indicate whether or not Lucy was cross-examined; if she was, the gist of the questions are unknown. Certainly, Pugh could have painted—and perhaps did paint—Lucy as an unreliable witness based on her incomplete testimony to the coroner's jury. But the damage was done. The jury had heard testimony that they could not unhear. It had been a far worse day than the first session of court, and the defense was likely relieved when they adjourned for the night.

The third day of court, however, would prove worse still.

As the usual throng filed early into the courtroom, jockeying for the best seats, the *Roanoke Times* reporter noted, with satisfaction, that many of them were carrying the morning paper and using it to refresh their memories of the previous day. The papers were quickly folded and put away, however, when Judge Griffin entered the courtroom just before 10:00 a.m. Soon afterward, the proceedings opened.

The first witness that day, Asa Jackson, told of seeing a man he believed to be Charles and a woman he scarcely noticed on the macadamized road near Gum Spring on the morning of the murder. The timing was important: Jackson said he saw the couple close to dawn of the day in question. It was not necessarily blockbuster testimony—Jackson seemed uncertain of the details and wouldn't definitively identify either person. He merely thought it might be Charles as he passed; the woman he couldn't even identify as black or white. But the jurors couldn't miss the inference. If it was Charles, and since Edith was still at the Watkins cabin at the time, the unidentified woman could only have been Susan.

If the geography was correct, however, it would mean that Charles and Susan passed the scene of the murder, went as far as the road and then returned in the direction of Gum Spring, where she met her demise. In retrospect, it seems an unlikely course of events. Still, Asa Jackson's testimony did the defense no favors.

The next witness called was a surprise: Frank Lovelock, the reporter for the *Roanoke Times* who had likely covered the case from the beginning. (The stories on the Watkins case never carried bylines, so it is impossible to be certain.) Lovelock had also served on the coroner's jury. Not surprisingly, the defense raised a swift objection: Lovelock had not been on the original witness list, and he had been in the courtroom from the start of the proceedings and so had heard prejudicial information. Commonwealth's Attorney Ballard looked surprised; he said that he had mentioned this witness to Pugh some time beforehand, and the other lawyer had expressed no objection then. After some discussion of the matter at the bench, Judge Griffin overruled the objection and allowed Lovelock to take the stand.

In the end, the reporter had little to offer, merely identifying clothing worn by Susan on her last day alive. After testifying, Lovelock was told to leave the courtroom, as other witnesses did. The *Times* must have had a second reporter on hand, as coverage of the proceedings continued.

Next to testify was Walter Boon, a Salem police officer who had been dispatched to Roanoke to collect the trunks of the dead woman as evidence. He identified the trunks and their contents for the court, especially noting the marriage certificate Susan had repeatedly mentioned as proof of who the real Mrs. Watkins was.

Once again, the defense raised an objection over a matter that seems a ridiculous technicality in retrospect. But courtroom procedure paid scrupulously close attention to technicalities, so the jury filed out while Griffin considered the objection carefully. The marriage certificate, Pugh observed, listed the groom's name as Charles Henry Watkins. But all of the court documents, including the indictment, did not use Charles's middle name, raising the fantastically remote chance of an error having been made. Perhaps some eyes rolled in the crowd of spectators, but the judge sustained the objection.

The jury returned, and—unusually—Lovelock was called back to the stand. He was asked to identify Susan's watch and some contents of the trunk, which, as a member of the coroner's inquest, he had seen months before. The final witness before the lunch break was a T.J. Wilson, who corroborated earlier testimony that Charles and Susan had boarded the streetcar in Roanoke together on April 6.

After the brief recess, the lawyers began a heated debate over the gold watch found with Susan's body. Although previous witnesses had identified it already, Pugh now objected that no proof had been offered that it was, indeed, Susan Watkins's watch. Griffin overruled the objection, stating the prior witness testimony had established the identity of the timepiece with reasonable certainty.

Ballard then called to the stand Mat Bailey, who shared a house with John Banks in Gum Spring. He told of hearing pistol shots in the night the previous April. Recognizing that evidence of Charles shooting his wife was, to say the least, damaging to his case, Pugh aggressively cross-examined Bailey, but to no avail. "By his earnestness and straightforward manner, he was able several times to get the better of the defense," reported the newspaper.

Observers in the courtroom may have become a little bored with the proceedings by then and were turning back to their newspapers. Witnesses mostly repeating details from the day before, tedious arguments over legal technicalities, lawyerly jargon and endless sotto voce conferences at the bench—this was not great theater, not that a courtroom is meant to cater to an audience.

But every ear perked up and a murmur ran through the crowd as Ballard called his next witness. This was what the spectators had been awaiting.

Ben Wright was now to take the stand.

As FAR BACK AS August, the *Roanoke Times* had reported that Ben Wright had been the recipient of the "fatal letter" that had resulted in Watkins's arrest. Some details of the contents had seemingly been leaked to the press, such as the otherwise unknown information that Charles hoped to escape to Europe and that there was an apparent confession in that envelope.

But the full contents of the letter had been seen by only a select few law enforcement authorities. Watkins's defense attorneys had not even seen it, and as far as can be known Charles had never admitted—and possibly did not remember—writing such a letter.

But of course, what was reported in the paper and what was circulating in local gossip circuits were two different things. Certainly, rumors were flying; rumormongers were spreading in hushed tones the usual mixture of truth and bald assumption. But equally certainly, all local scuttlebutt for months must have been anticipating the testimony of Cousin Ben, the man who knew more about the crime than anyone else, save the perpetrator, the one who had blown the stalled case wide open. He would tell his story; the entire Roanoke Valley wanted to hear what he had to say.

Wright's testimony began with narrative, crucial details in the story of murder William Ballard was trying to write for the jury. He told of the unexpected arrival at his door of Susan, claiming to be the wife of his cousin; he recounted the eventful trek to Roanoke to confront her wayward spouse. Much of what he had to say had already been heard in the testimony of George and Phyllis Washington, so was more corroborative than explosive information.

But then Ballard asked the key question: Did Wright have any communication from Charles Watkins in the weeks he was a fugitive from justice? Ballard was, of course, following the lawyer's maxim for testimony: never ask a question if you don't already know the answer.

Yes, Ben replied. He had received a letter.

There was probably no gasp from the spectators in the courtroom, as anyone who had followed the case closely already knew the letter existed. But it's not hard to imagine people leaning forward in their seats, straining to hear every syllable.

Pulling an envelope from a stack of papers, Ballard showed it to the witness: "Is this the letter?"

"It is," Ben Wright replied.

Ballard, anticipating the defense strategy of challenging the origin of the letter, asked the witness if he recognized the penmanship. Ben assured the court that he was quite familiar with his cousin's handwriting, having had letters from him through the years he was "out west." It will also be remembered that in the coroner's inquest, long before the letter was written, Ben had asserted that he knew Charles' handwriting and recognized it on letters Susan had showed him.

Wright then added another detail, a piece of the story undisclosed until that moment. The Sunday after Charles had arrived in Salem in custody, he sent a message to his cousin Ben through Charles Hatcher, who was at the jail for some purpose. Ben came to the jail and stood outside, speaking with Charles through the window of the cell, Deputy Hening listening in on the conversation.

"Charles asked me did I receive a letter from him in North Carolina," Wright recounted. "I told him I did, and he said he was sorry he had ever written it." Again, it seems that Charles had little recollection of sending the letter that was about to seal his fate. Or at least he was unwilling to admit to such.

At this point, understandably, the defense attorneys objected to entering the letter as evidence, most obviously objecting that they had not seen the contents of the letter. They could not effectively defend their client under such a circumstance, and Griffin could only agree. The letter was given to the defense to peruse. Pugh, Moffett and McClung huddled over the letter, digesting the contents with growing alarm. This was bad. Very bad. Every effort to exclude the letter had to be made.

At length, Pugh announced that the defense had several objections to the letter, and the jury was led out of the room. The full substance of Pugh's objections was not reported in the papers, but Wright's ability to recognize the letter as from Charles was a key point. After much discussion, Judge Griffin ruled that the letter could be admitted as evidence and read in its entirety to the jury.

The jury returned, and Wright was cross-examined by the defense. Wright was aggressively asked about his certainty that the letter came from Charles, Pugh hoping that a glimmer of doubt might be shown to the jurors—but to no avail. Benjamin Wright stuck unwaveringly to his story.

Finally, Ballard picked up the letter, and, in a clear voice, read the text to the courtroom, the first time the contents had been made public. Both the *Roanoke Times* and the *Salem Times-Register* published "word for word" accounts the next day, preserving the momentous epistle for history:

Wilmington, NC
July 4, 1891

Dear Cousin Ben:

I no that you are my friend if there is any one on earth; you all ways have been, Ben. Dear Sir, you no the trouble I am in, but you don't no why I got into this trouble and how it was. I will tell you all about it. I no you was the cause of me doing what I did. I will forgive you because you was not thinking. If you had come to Roanoke and inform me of the trouble I was about to get in I would of taken Ida and went about my business, but you taken this old lady and brought her on me in a respectful family without me noing a word about it. Oh, I do think this will kill me. I don't think I will ever get over it. Ben, I have been every place to get away from this woman, but she followed me all over the country. If she had been any thing it would of been different thing, but I will tell you the truth about it.

She has threaten my life 20 times. She waited one night in Chicago all night for me to go to sleep so she could shoot me, and drawed a pistol on me when she thought I was sleep in the night and I caught her hand, Bennie. She told me the night I went home with her in the country, she says "I intend to kill you and Ida before I go back to Chicago"; also she says to me "if I don't kill you I will kill Ida if I will be hung the next moment." Bennie, I had to do something to save my life and Ida also. I would not give Ida for one thousand women like the one I killed. I wanted to get away without any trouble with her, but I did not see how I could get away from her.

Ben, I would not tell a lie for nothing and I can prove this by Chicago people. She is nothing and I ought to be shot for fooling my time away with such a woman as she was. I got mix up with her and I could not get way from her. She has cost me 1,000 dollars while I was gone from home 8 years.

She did not have any character whatever. I no she filled you up talking. Ben, I will have cause myself to be in much danger on the account of keeping bad company. Ben, I do hate to leave Ida behind, but there was a friend of mine in Roanoke despatch to me and says "go as fast as cars can carry you; Ida is lock up in jail, and if you can get away they can't do anything with her."

Then started a foot walk, two hundred miles, and then I was nearly dead, so I got on the train and rode until all my money was gone, rings, overcoat, pistol and everything else. Ben, I look like a tramp. I have nothing. I am going to cross the ocean Atlantic. Whenever I can hear from you tell me where is Ida. Ben, don't tell nobody that you have heard from me, not even your wife. Ben, you don't want to see me hung dead by the neck for ____ [apparently unreadable]. *Ben, I no you are the only friend I have on earth.*

Bennie, stand by me until I can get across Atlantic ocean; then I will be safe. Now, cousin, don't tell nobody that you have heard from me again. Ben, burn this up for my sake. Bennie, I am not guilty in this case. Write in haste to me. I have changed my name. Direct mail to Wilmington, NC, PO to S.G. Williams. That is the name I am going by since I left Salem. Bennie, please do anything you can for me when I am in trouble.

I will write you a long letter next time; tell you my troubles.

But Charles had already told his troubles and made a stark, unmissable, irredeemable confession: *"I would not give Ida for one thousand women like the one I killed."*

The reaction of the courtroom was described by the *Roanoke Times* the next day:

After the reading of this letter there was a deathly and impressive silence. The prisoner's face, now a ghastly yellow, twitched with emotion and suppressed feelings—he evidently realized that his chances for life and liberty were utterly gone. The countenances of his lawyers were almost an amusing study, for it seem to many that they were temporarily nonplussed; while the face of the commonwealth's attorney bore a quiet, satisfied smile. He knew that the letter, written by the prisoner and acknowledging his guilt so freely and fully, had sealed his doom.

Ben Wright, the star witness, was dismissed, and disappears from the remainder of the drama. The role he played could not have been an easy one for him. He had, in effect, placed his cousin's neck in a noose—or perhaps more accurately, had declined to hide the noose Charles had placed around his own neck.

But he had done the right thing, turning material evidence of a crime over to law enforcement, then telling the court the truth, the whole truth and nothing but the truth. Judge Griffin, in perhaps a backhanded way, would commend Ben Wright at the end of the trial for bringing the letter to light. Speaking to Charles, Griffin said that had Benjamin Wright "through some whimsical and ill-founded scruples, failed in his duty as a citizen of this Commonwealth, to communicate to the officers of the law the evidence he possessed of your guilt, given by you in a letter to him, he would have been unworthy of the protection which the law is established to afford—that those who 'walk uprightly may walk safely;' that 'they who do no harm may feel none.'"

If there is a hero to this story, it was the blacksmith Benjamin Wright, a man with an unwavering moral compass, a man who did as much as anyone else to see justice done for Susan Wilson Watkins.

LATE IN THE AFTERNOON, the testimony of former sheriff Charles Webber and current sheriff George Zirkle was heard, both describing aspects of the manhunt for Watkins. Lovelock and Hatcher were also recalled to clarify some points related to the possessions in Susan's trunk, and a Mr. Compton, who occasionally worked at the jail, told the story of taking a letter from Charles Watkins, at the prisoner's request, to the *Salem Times-Register*. Finally, Gardner Hickok, an employee of the paper, described this same letter. These last two witnesses were perhaps intended by the prosecution to establish other persons who had seen Watkins's handwriting, although Compton conceded that he was not particularly familiar with the defendant's penmanship.

No matter. As the court adjourned at 5:20 p.m., the chance of Watkins's acquittal had been severely diminished, if not demolished. Ballard had presented a masterful case against the accused, with the defendant's own words in the "fatal letter" forming the capstone.

It seems the Charles Watkins was aware of his dire predicament, if a report in the *Roanoke Times* later in the week is to be believed. Arriving back at the jail on that Wednesday afternoon, Charles was said to send for an unnamed member of jailer Hening's family, who had previously "shown him many acts of kindness." Charles confided to this visitor that he would never have thought his cousin Ben would have turned the letter over to the authorities and that having heard his own words in court, he had "given up all hope."

But the trial was not concluded yet. It still remained to be seen what sort of defense the stellar legal minds of Pugh, Moffett and McClung could, against all odds, present to the court.

9

"Death Trap Ready"

Pastor Benjamin Fox tried again to concentrate on his prayer list, but this confounded necktie wasn't cooperating. He pulled the one end back through the knot to try again.

An elderly parishioner had given him the tie as a Christmas gift a year or two ago, and she liked to see him wear it when he visited her. Since hers was one of the names on the prayer list, and since he had anticipated preaching her funeral before much more time passed, he was happy to make her happy. Even if the cravat was stiff and difficult to knot properly. He fussed over the knot again, and then again. Finally, he decided it looked passable, but it was tight around his collar, almost like a silken noose.

The thought of a noose reminded him of another name on the prayer list, and another visit—to the jail—to make this morning. He had never known the prisoner Charles Watkins—Fox had arrived in Salem after Charles had left the state. Fled the state with policemen on his heels, the local gossip claimed. But he knew some of his relations in passing and was familiar with the man's case. In fact, he had preached the murdered woman's funeral the previous spring.

Fox considered visiting the jail his duty as a Christian, whether or not he was a pastor. Working for the benefit of a soul as tortured as Watkins's was a privilege. After all, hadn't Jesus likened himself to a hopeless convict in Matthew 25? "I was in prison and you came to Me." When Fox paid a call on the disagreeable condemned man, he was ministering to the "least of these" as his Lord commanded.

But Fox did not relish the visit later in the day. When he had first called at the man's cell in company with another local pastor, Watkins had been receptive, interested, eager to sing familiar hymns with his surprisingly good bass voice. Representatives of the Salvation Army also paid him visits, and he seemed appreciative. He had even made a profession of religion, though Fox wasn't convinced. He had been in the pastoring business long enough to know that a man in dire straits was not always sincere in such professions. And Watkins was in the direst of straits—listening daily to the hammer strokes as workmen built the gallows on which he would die.

But more recently, Watkins had suddenly become belligerent, insulting, even blasphemous. Some folks around town surmised that he was shamming insanity, trying to get his sentence changed. Fox couldn't say and didn't concern himself with such gossip. A prisoner's ravings did not change a pastor's responsibility to seek the spiritual betterment of a man in Charles's predicament. He would go, he would read some verses, he would pray for the man.

But one thing was certain—it wouldn't be as uplifting a visit as calling on his elderly parishioner would be afterward.

Pastor Benjamin Fox reached for his topcoat, preparing to step out into the wintry air. But then he stopped, yanked the knot out of his necktie and started fussing with it again.

THE FOURTH DAY OF the Watkins murder trial began with a bit of a surprise. Commonwealth's Attorney William Ballard announced unexpectedly that he rested his case. After all, Ben Wright's testimony the day before and the reading of the letter from Wilmington had established the guilt of the accused beyond the shadow of a doubt, it seemed to the prosecution. What more could be added?

At the defense table, Arthur Pugh hesitated for a moment. He stood and confessed he had not been prepared to offer his testimony immediately in the day's proceedings and asked Judge Griffin for a brief recess to confer with his client and the other defense attorneys. The request was granted, and (accompanied by the jailer for security) Watkins and his counselors retreated to a vacant jury room to strategize.

Twenty minutes later, court reconvened, and Pugh called his first witness. He had to try to demolish the case of the prosecution, but it soon became evident that the weapons in his arsenal were meager at best.

The first person called for the defense was Addie Anderson, cousin of the accused, and still deemed the "Delinquent Witness" by the *Roanoke Times* for her initial failure to appear in court earlier in the week. She had originally been described as a crucial witness for both defense and prosecution, yet Ballard had never called her.

Little of what Addie testified survives in the press accounts of the trial—perhaps the newspapers, convinced the outcome of the trial was over with Wright's testimony, saw no need to give much attention to the defense witnesses. The bulk of her testimony dealt with chronology—when the body was found, when she arrived at Gum Spring that same evening. Perhaps the most relevant evidence she gave was to report a conversation that night with Lucy Watkins. Addie asked if Charles had brought a woman with him on the night before the murder, and Lucy replied, "No. God in Heaven knows he did not bring her with him." As related earlier, this was technically true—Charles arrived at the Watkins cabin alone. But this was hardly enough to refute the earlier testimony of Taylor and Lucy that Susan was certainly at their home that fateful night.

Addie was "slightly cross-examined" by Ballard and told to step down. Despite all of the court's perturbation at her absence on Monday, little that she said on Thursday seemed to shape the outcome of the case. But it's clear what the defense was attempting: to cast some slight doubt on the idea that Charles and Susan were ever on the mountain together.

The next witness may have given Ballard a little more pause, but it didn't last for long. Professor Orren L. Stearnes took the stand. A graduate of Richmond College and a former teacher at the Allegheny Institute in Roanoke, Stearnes was called to cast doubt on the key piece of evidence for the prosecution: the "fatal letter." Under oath, Stearnes testified that Ben Wright could not possibly have been able to identify his cousin's handwriting, not after spending a decade apart and receiving only a couple of letters from him in that interval.[31]

This was potentially damaging testimony to the prosecution case, so much of which rested on the letter in question. But Ballard quickly and cleanly dealt with the witness. Raising an objection, the prosecution asked if Stearnes was a recognized expert in forensic analysis of penmanship or the ability of individuals to identify it. Stearnes (then employed as a realtor) conceded that he was in no way such an expert, merely expressing his opinion. Accordingly, Ballard asked that this evidence be stricken from the record, and Griffin sustained the objection.

Pugh had bluffed. Ballard had called the bluff. Game over.

Next, Pugh recalled Taylor Watkins to the stand, asking him to clarify some points of chronology, especially when he left for work on the morning of the murder. Again, it seems that Pugh was trying to establish doubt about Charles's proximity in time and place to the murder scene, but there was no blockbuster revelation in Taylor's testimony—only adding to his previous testimony that he thought he'd mentioned Charles's visit to a coworker the next morning. It was nothing Pugh could use. The witness was excused and stepped down.

"May it please your honor, we rest our case here," Pugh announced. If the prosecutor smiled to himself in satisfaction, it is not recorded.

Ballard had taken three days to present his case. Pugh was done in little over an hour. Three witnesses: one dismissed, the other two hardly challenging the rampart of evidence the prosecution had assembled. "The evidence for the defense [was] very meager," noted the *Roanoke Times* the next day, not usually a paragon of understatement.

CLOSING ARGUMENTS FOR BOTH sides remained, but an issue within the jury was a growing concern. R.H. Rhodes, one of the jurors, was sick and growing worse by the moment. At least two other jurors were also feeling ill—possibly with flu, or "the grip" in the parlance of the day. The papers would speak that month of an outbreak of influenza in the Roanoke Valley. The last thing Judge Griffin wanted was to delay the trial further due to illness, and he encouraged the jurors to tough it out. While the panel took a short break, the attorneys debated among themselves the particulars of the instructions to the jury.

At 12:15 p.m., the jurors returned, and Ballard commenced with his summation. This was his chance to wrap up the days of testimony for the jury and help them to interpret it—in a way favorable to his case, of course.

With dramatic flourish, Major Ballard recounted for the court the undisputed facts of the murder and the sensational discovery of Susan's body in the creek at Gum Spring. Everyone, he noted, began to ask who could have perpetrated such a deed, and "with a unanimity unparalleled, Charles Watkins was pronounced to be the man."

Ballard diverted his train of thought to explain to the jury the legal distinctions between first- and second-degree murder, then returned to the facts of the case. He summarized the findings of the surgeons who performed the autopsy and noted the inescapable fact that Charles Watkins was the last man seen with Susan and that it had been firmly established that he was in the vicinity of the crime scene on the day of the murder.

Then, he turned to the question of motive and took the jury back to Susan's arrival at Ben Wright's house, followed the next day by her unexpected appearance at the Washingtons' boardinghouse. This established motive, Ballard opined—Charles had to eliminate this inconvenient wife to keep his illicit relationship with Ida.

Next, he took the jury on the journey from Roanoke to Salem and then to the banks of the creek alongside Fannie Coxe's home. Here the prosecutor stopped and picked up the previous day's *Roanoke Times*, much to the delight of the reporter in attendance. Ballard began to quote from the paper, but Judge Griffin stopped him short—he should stick to his own notes, His Honor instructed. But then Griffin took note of the time and decided to call a recess for lunch.

An hour later, at 2:15 p.m., court reconvened. Rhodes, the most ill of the sick jurors, was allowed to recline on a lounge to hear the rest of the case. But he was determined to proceed.

Ballard continued his closing, painting Susan as a pitiable victim, "deserted by the man who should have protected her." With "descriptive eloquence," the Commonwealth's Attorney followed the wounded woman to the porch of Taylor Watkins's cabin and then to her departure with Charles the next morning, never to be seen alive again.

To be sure the jury kept the primary evidence in mind, he reread the "Wilmington Letter," with its unmistakable confession by the defendant. Ballard then closed by defining for the jury such legal definitions as malice aforethought and circumstantial evidence. He reminded the jury of its duty to consider the evidence and decide which side had met the standard of "beyond a reasonable doubt."

Ballard sat down, confident that he had made the prosecution's case. Now the defense would have its turn.

CLOSING ARGUMENTS FOR THE defense began with Marshall McClung, the junior partner of Watkins's team of lawyers. Young, but a compelling speaker, McClung decided to win the jury over with some lighthearted humor, poking fun at Ballard. Exactly what he said did not make it into the press coverage, but his intention seems clear. If he could cause the jury to view the prosecution case as only a big joke, perhaps they would side with his client. Perhaps.

But the defense needed more—to undermine the facts of the case against Charles. McClung called to the attention of the jury certain small inconsistencies in testimony, facts that were exaggerated or misrepresented by witnesses. The paper failed to explain what these facts were but described them as immaterial to the overall case. "It is doubtful if he succeeded in removing from the minds of the jury any of those important points which seem so thoroughly to fasten the guilt upon the prisoner," the *Roanoke Times* concluded.

By the time McClung was finished, it was 8:10 in the evening, and Griffin adjourned the court for the night. Defense arguments would have to continue the next day.

COURT RECONVENED THE NEXT morning, November 20, with the usual punctuality. Defense Attorney William Walter Moffett would now take center stage in the drama, directing his keen legal mind and acknowledged oratorical ability to the dismantling of the prosecution case. It would be, certainly, no easy task.

Congratulating and flattering the jury for its perseverance (especially given that two ailing jurors were now reclining on lounges rather than sitting in the jury box), Moffett hinged his closing argument on the nature of the given testimony and the proper consideration of circumstantial evidence. "I do not say there is no such thing as circumstantial evidence," proclaimed

William Walter Moffett. *Salem Historical Society.*

Moffett, "for if I did you would not believe me, nor would I be respected as I hope I deserve. There is circumstantial evidence, but it must be from a chain that does not lack a connecting link. And in this case I claim that there are missing links."

In other words, Moffett hoped to convince the jury none of the evidence presented in a week of trial testimony could conclusively prove Charles Watkins a murderer. As much as the body of evidence might seem to propel a jury to such a conclusion, the "missing links" were enough to cast doubt on the prosecution's version of events.

Among the claims that Moffett eloquently laid before the jury, he asserted:

- The scene of the murder was in actuality a well-traveled place, not an out-of-the-way "lonely spot."
- Charles did not leave the cabin of his uncle until soon before the body was found in the creek—not with the haste of a guilty man.
- While Charles had been seen with a woman in Roanoke and Salem the evening before the murder, no one could irrefutably prove that woman's identity.
- Charles had not been proven to have been "within 400 yards of the place she was murdered."
- Fannie Coxe could not identify the woman she saw given the failing light of the April evening.
- "Murderers do not want light," and so Charles, had he been plotting a homicide, would hardly have borrowed a lantern from the Coxe sisters.
- While testimony had been presented that Susan had been shot in the hand, no medical examination had mentioned such a wound on the body found in Horner's Branch.[32]
- There was no evidence to suggest that Charles had harbored murderous thoughts toward his estranged wife.
- Asa Jackson's testimony that he saw Charles in the company of an unidentified woman on the morning of the murder was too vague to draw definite conclusions.
- Ben Wright could not possibly identify the handwriting of his cousin on the "fatal letter" after so long an absence from each other. If Charles made mention of a letter to Ben while in jail, it could have been a different one. In fact, Moffett hinted that the letter shown and read in court could have been substituted for a more innocent missive—a rather conspiratorial interpretation of the facts.

But perhaps most incredibly, Moffett suggested that the body found in the creek had not been conclusively identified as that of Susan Watkins at all. Obviously, it followed that her husband could hardly be convicted of her murder if she was not, in fact, proven dead. It was a far-fetched theory, to be sure, and doubtlessly was given little credence by the jurors.

For the sake of his client's defense, Moffett was ignoring the fact that Susan's body had been identified immediately after its discovery. While the exact means of establishing her identity were not described, it stands to reason that the Wrights, the Watkins and Washingtons could attest to her name and appearance. Phyllis Washington had testified that she did exactly that.

Perhaps to the modern observer, Moffett might have had a point. Tried-and-true identification methods with which our age is familiar—fingerprinting, dental records, DNA testing—did not yet exist. But if the body found was not Susan's, the jurors must have thought, two questions would have to be answered. First, who was she? No other person had been reported missing. Gum Spring was not the sort of place where strangers frequently wandered anonymously to their peril. The bodies of unidentified, well-dressed urbanite strangers did not routinely materialize in Roanoke County creeks.

Second, if someone else had been found dead in the stream, where was Susan? No one had seen her since the morning of the murder. Her two trunks containing all of her earthly possessions had not been claimed. No one had contacted authorities and reported that Susan Wilson Watkins had been seen alive and well somewhere else.

The spurious claim that the murdered woman was unidentified was tenuous at best, laughable at worst. One wonders if Moffett wasn't a trifle embarrassed to even suggest such a bizarre theory.

MOFFETT'S WHOLE ARGUMENT, TAKING up three hours of court time, hinged on the fact (which was not denied by the prosecution) that there was no eyewitness to the crime. All the evidence then was inevitably circumstantial in nature, but that did not make it less convincing. Circumstantial evidence was not immaterial and could certainly lead to a guilty verdict. Unwittingly, Moffett may have admitted as much by making a reference to another well-known Virginia murder case. In a "passing allusion," Moffett invoked a familiar name that likely made the jurors' ears perk up—a name which, however, probably did little to help his case.

He brought into the Watkins case the specter of one Thomas Cluverius and his "celebrated watch key."

ON THE MORNING OF March 14, 1885, a watchman discovered the body of a young woman floating in the city reservoir in Richmond. She was recently dead, showed signs of an assault and was approximately eight months pregnant. Since she was unidentified, her body was laid out in a public chapel, and thousands of Richmond residents filed by her, ostensibly to attempt an identification, but more likely to gawk. Moffett had recently completed his term in the Virginia legislature and conceivably was himself in the city to follow the case.

After some false leads, the deceased was identified as Lillian Madison, a teacher estranged from her family in King William County. It did not take long to link her and her unborn child to her cousin Thomas Judson Cluverius. Cluverius, a popular and respected attorney and Sunday school teacher, was soon arrested for the murder.

Cluverius's trial became one of the most closely followed murder cases in Virginia history and was carefully dissected by attorneys because it dealt entirely with circumstantial evidence, there being no eyewitness to the crime. While the defendant maintained his innocence, prosecutors hammered away at his character and the scandalous relationship with his cousin. One of the key pieces of evidence was a watch key found near the reservoir. It fit Cluverius's pocket watch, which was missing its key.

Cluverius was found guilty and, despite many pleas for clemency, was hanged in Richmond on January 14, 1887.[33] The case became something of a precedent for Virginia's legal system on the uses of circumstantial evidence in murder cases.

There were obvious comparisons between the Cluverius and Watkins cases. Both seemed to involve an attempt by a man to rid himself of an inconvenient partner, both involved a betrayed woman discovered lifeless in a body of water, both drew immense public attention, both relied entirely on indirect evidence. This is why it was unusual, and arguably a mistake, for Moffett to mention the name Cluverius, even in passing.

Why remind the jury of a celebrated case in which the accused was hanged based only on circumstantial evidence?

While it seems unlikely that Moffett's small gaffe decisively swayed any juror, his allusion to it certainly could not have helped the defense case.

AFTER A LUNCH BREAK, it was time for lead defense attorney Arthur Benton Pugh to state his case, summing up the argument that his client was innocent, or at least that the case for guilt had not been proven.

Pugh was a capable attorney. He knew how to read a jury and how to lead a jury. While his partners had been arguing, Pugh had certainly been watching the jurors, looking for any reaction that might reveal where the case stood in their minds. A change of expression, a stifled yawn, a cocked eyebrow—did any of it mean anything? If so, he had one chance to try to exploit any uncertainty he had noticed.

Pugh began, like his associates, by praising the jury for its perseverance over the course of a long trial. He succinctly summed up the arguments of McClung and Moffett, reminding them of the circumstantial nature of the case. There was, he declared with dramatic redundancy, "not one particle of a scintilla of evidence to prove that there is any positive proof" of his client's guilt.

Some of Pugh's arguments were tenuous at best: "Charles Watkins, I claim, has not been shown by the evidence to have been any nearer the body found dead than the City of Roanoke," he boldly stated. Such an assertion not only ignored the testimony of multiple witnesses, but it also seemed to contradict Moffett's claim earlier in the day that the dead woman was not Susan Watkins. Pugh would seem to be saying that she was Susan after all, but Charles had not seen her since they were together in Roanoke.

The day was growing late. The reporter for the *Roanoke Times* seemed to tire of recording Pugh's statements in much detail, only summing up broad themes. Pugh clearly (and understandably) sought to impeach the testimony of the prosecution's witnesses, for instance suggesting that the woman seen by Fannie Coxe at the log bridge with Charles was in fact Ida Friebel.

He also savagely attacked the prosecution's prime evidence: the letter to Ben Wright. It was "unworthy of the importance attached to it by the prosecution," Pugh informed the jurors. He couldn't easily make the jury unhear the contents of the letter. But maybe he could cause them to ignore it.

Pugh's main goal, however, was not to undermine the substance of the evidence, but its nature. The circumstantial evidence heard in the trial, he asserted, was insufficient to hang a murder conviction on his client. Slyly, he tried to get the jury to decide that Charles Watkins may not be innocent, but the case against him had not been made. It was a subtle, and difficult, needle to thread.

Finally, Pugh concluded his closing and sat down. It was about 4:30 in the afternoon. He had done a masterful job in defending his client with eloquence, "command[ing] the admiration of all who heard him," the *Times* reported.

Ballard asked for, and got, a chance to correct some points of evidence he believed Pugh had misquoted, which only took a few minutes. With that, Pugh, Moffett and McClung had concluded their defense case. They had been dealt a difficult hand in this game, but they adroitly played the cards they were dealt, making the best case they could for a difficult client. Three capable attorneys had spent hours mustering every argument, every interpretation of the evidence, every possible reevaluation of all that the witnesses had said, resolutely seeking to convince at least one juror that Charles Watkins was not guilty. Was it enough?

The *Salem Times-Register* gave little specific coverage of the defense's closing arguments. The weekly paper merely printed this quick, brutal synopsis: "Nearly the whole of Friday was passed by the jury in listening to the able speeches of Messrs. Pugh and Moffett, who did all that could be done by these talented lawyers to save the neck of an unworthy client."

The time had come for the jury to do its work. Earlier in the trial, the two sides had spent some time arguing and haggling over the precise instructions that the court would give the jury to guide its deliberations. The jury instructions were just words, but words are exactly that over which lawyers are trained to argue. At length, both sides had settled on this formulation:

> *No. 1: The court instructs the jury that if from the evidence in the case they have any reasonable doubt of the guilt of the prisoner, Charles Watkins, as charged in the indictment, they must find him not guilty.*
>
> *No. 2: The court further instructs the jury* [that] *if from the evidence in the case they have any reasonable doubt as to any important fact necessary to convict the prisoner of the offense charged in the indictment, they are bound to give the prisoner the benefit of that doubt.*
>
> *No. 3: The court instructs the jury that unless they believe from the evidence in this case, to a moral certainty and beyond all reasonable doubt, that the dead body found was* [Susan Watkins], *then they cannot find him guilty.*[34]

Pugh and his team had carefully crafted these instructions around their defense strategy and, in turn, wove their closing arguments around the instructions. They needed only a reasonable sliver of doubt. Ballard, much more confident in his case, was fine with the final list. The evidence presented would speak for itself. Now these instructions would be put to the test.

After days of testimony and courtroom theatrics and lawyerly rhetoric, the twelve men of the jury stood and filed out of the courtroom after Sheriff Zirkle, climbing a flight of stairs to a secure room to begin deliberations.

For both the prosecution and the defense, a waiting game began. There was never any way of knowing how long jury deliberations would

Sheriff George W. Zirkle.
Roanoke County Libraries.

take. Certainly, there was a lot of evidence to consider. The spectators—the gallery was still full of onlookers taking in the show—whispered among themselves with idle speculations. The attorneys turned over the case in their minds, trying to see it as the jury would. And as for Charles, who had sat impassively at his place all week, betraying little emotion, he "for the first time during the day moved uneasily in his seat, and looked anxious and even scared." His fate was being decided by twelve strangers in the room above.

A waiting game. And then, suddenly, shockingly quickly, it was over.

The jurors returned to the courtroom and took their places. Judge Griffin asked if they had reached a verdict. "We have," the foreman replied.

"Guilty."

It had taken all of twenty-one minutes.

THERE WERE NOW FORMALITIES. Griffin ordered Watkins to stand and had the clerk read the written verdict to him. To no one's surprise, Pugh then stood and made a motion for a new trial, asking Griffin to set aside the verdict. The judge, understanding all too well how the game was played, agreed to hear the defense appeal the next morning, although it meant an unusual Saturday session of the county court. Should the appeal fail, the convicted murderer would then be sentenced.

Griffin turned his attention to the jury, dismissing them with his thanks:

> *Gentlemen of the jury, the court, before discharging you, wishes to express its appreciation of the patient manner in which you have borne the ordeal through which you have passed in the trial of this case, as evidenced by the sickness of several of your members.*
>
> *You will return to your homes, I doubt not, gentlemen, with consciences satisfied that you have discharged your duty as jurors and as citizens, and that, therefore, no regrets can ever follow you.*
>
> *Hoping that those of you now so much indisposed will be soon restored to perfect health, you are discharged.*

The Saturday session of the Roanoke County Court saw as large a crowd of spectators as the previous days had seen. Pugh and the defense team had one last, remote, chance, of keeping the noose from around the neck of Charles Watkins.

The modern observer of court proceedings, accustomed to appeals in capital cases that may last for years, will find the literal rush to judgment keenly unfamiliar. Pugh, Moffett and McClung had the evening of November 20 to prepare their case for reversing their client's guilty plea, but they did not expect anything else. They understood by then that Judge Wingfield Griffin would brook no legal shenanigans and would grant no lengthy continuances.

Still, when the court convened, Pugh implored the bench to give the defense a short recess to complete their preparations. Griffin ordered a recess until 2:00 p.m., at which time the attorneys were to be ready—or as ready as they would be—to proceed.

Pugh did the speaking. Few details survive of his arguments for a new trial, but it is known (from the brief *Roanoke Times* coverage) that he based his appeal on three points. First, he claimed that the body had not been definitively identified as that of Susan Wilson Watkins. Second, he challenged the court's jurisdiction, as no one had proven that the crime in question had been committed in Roanoke County (although obviously the body had been found there). Finally, he made a technical legal objection to the way the grand jury indictment from the previous July had been presented in court, leaving a sliver of doubt about whether the defendant had been properly charged.

Griffin listened patiently to Pugh's objections and certainly weighed them in his mind, silently determining if there was any legitimacy to these objections. But when Pugh concluded, the judge wasted no time in rendering his verdict.

Without hesitation, he overruled each of the points. The appeal had failed. There would be no new trial. The verdict would stand. Charles Watkins remained a convicted wife murderer.

Next, Judge Griffin asked Charles to stand, and his attorneys stood with him. The verdict from the previous day was read again to the defendant. The judge asked if he had anything to say as to why the court should not pass judgment upon him. Charles whispered a moment to his attorneys, and then "without flinching, in a firm voice, replied that he had nothing to say." He sat.

The time for judgment had arrived. Griffin also was unflinching, speaking in "calm, unmodulated tones." As a jurist, he had sentenced many people to varying degrees of punishment, but he had never presided over a case like this. He certainly felt the gravity of his duty and made a short speech[35] to make clear the judgment of the court. He had, he said,

> *no desire, nor will* [I] *further harrow your feelings by recurring to the horrors of the crime for which you stand convicted by a fair and impartial jury of your countrymen; and that, after an exceptionally able defense of you by your counsel. Though the crime was committed when, so far as we know, no human eyes but your own witnessed it, and before its commission, therefore, you may have thought it would be safe in your keeping, still that conscience which for wise purposes has been implanted in us all by Providence, led you to confess your fearful and diabolical deed.*

Griffin went on to speak of the "fatal letter" sent to Ben Wright as the key piece of evidence. "Your conscious guilt, contrary to your expectations, no doubt confounded your faculties, and, to gain sympathy and commiseration without which you confessedly could not live, you confided your fatal secret to your hitherto friend." But the sentence he was about to pronounce was not merely a result of that one letter: "Your confession aside, the evidence in this case, in the opinion of the court, was full, satisfactory and all sufficient to warrant the verdict of the jury."

Griffin may have paused a moment, steeling himself for what must come.

> *The jury in their verdict having found you guilty of murder in the first degree, the order of the court is that you shall be hanged by the neck until you are dead; and that execution of this judgment be made and done upon you, Charles Watkins, by the Sheriff of this county, on Friday, the eighth day of January, 1892, between the hours of ten in the forenoon, and four in the afternoon of the same day, at the place of execution and in the manner determined by law.*

The trial was over. The condemned man remained impassive, detached, betraying no emotion as he heard his fate sealed. The crowd also was silent, finding no joy in the moment, only solemnity. Watkins stood and was led for the last time out of the courtroom and back to the jail, the grounds of which he would never again leave.

The convicted wife murderer had forty-seven days to live.

"THE PENALTY FOR HIS BRUTAL CRIME"

John Thomason shivered and shoved his hands deeper into his overcoat's pockets as he filed out into the yard from the treasurer's office, where a few dozen men had been waiting in the crowded warmth. Looking across at the tall structure in the fenced compound, he wondered once again why he had come to this spectacle. He glanced around at the gathered crowd and wondered if he should leave the way he had come. No one would think less of him if he did. Yet he stayed rooted to the spot.

It was some days ago that he'd been asked by the sheriff if he'd like one of the few tickets available to the public, and he'd impulsively said yes. But almost immediately he began to have his doubts. Tickets to a hanging—the first in Salem since 1880—were rare, and he knew several people who had hopes of gaining admission within the walled enclosure behind the jail. He could hear people milling about outside the tall fence, hoping to see something of the proceedings.

Thomason was neither a particularly squeamish man nor opposed to capital punishment, yet the idea of watching a man die bothered him a little. He scanned the crowd to see if his friend Watts Dillard had changed his mind and decided to come. The condemned man himself had requested the druggist attend, for reasons no one could tell. Dillard had known the man his whole life, but why his presence had been requested was a mystery. But then, the prisoner was said to be out of his head.

When he'd brought the ticket around, the sheriff had said that Dillard may attend. Thomason's jewelry store was only a few doors from Dillard's drugstore, and the two chatted often. So he'd strolled up to talk to him about it, but Doc just shook his head. No, he had no desire to go. He'd seen Hawley hanged back in '80, and that was enough to last his lifetime. But he didn't try to talk Thomason out of attending.

Like everyone else he knew, Thomason had followed the case closely in the local papers. He also knew the man. Only a short while before the crime, Charles had come into the store to introduce Thomason to his white "wife," whom he had greeted politely but reservedly. They were an odd couple, certainly. Yet the jeweler never would have suspected the man to be capable of such a crime. At the same time, he had no doubt about his guilt or the correctness of the verdict.

So here he was, in the chilly bright sunshine of a January morning, waiting, along with a hundred or more of his neighbors—invited spectators, court officials, reporters and the selected jury—to see the sentence was indeed carried out. He had deliberately positioned himself near the back of the rows of spectators, as far from the gallows as he could be and still be in attendance. Thomason felt his stomach quiver in nervousness, increasingly fascinated and disturbed by the whole affair.

There was a murmur in the crowd, and Thomason realized the condemned man was being brought out. He caught a glimpse of the man in a smart black suit with a cap on his head—he realized the cap had a veil. When the moment came, it would be draped over Watkins's face. His hands were cuffed together and pinioned to his waist. He was quiet but seemed to walk in a bit of an understandable daze.

After that, the crowd before him obstructed Thomason's view. He could see the sheriff, the deputy, Pastor Fox and the condemned atop the gallows, but he realized that when the trap sprang he'd not be able to see beneath. That didn't bother him in the least.

He could hear though. He heard the man's blasphemous ravings and then a short silence. And then a moment later the sound he'd remember the rest of his life.

The sound like a heavy log being dropped on a woodhouse floor.[36]

The end of the trial did not mean the end of the public fascination with the case of Charles Watkins. Gossip continued to fly; reporters continued to lurk around the jail hoping to overhear some tidbit to share with their readers.

At Roanoke College, the main building of which was only one hundred yards from the courthouse, interest in the case was keen among the student body. In the December issue of the *Roanoke Collegian*, the campus newspaper for the all-male school, it was noted that "the boys were very much interested in the Watkins trial, and many were the comments made, and many 'if *I* were a lawyer' suggestions." It was also noted that a student named Stirewalt had "made the best point when he said that he didn't see how they could convict Watkins of *manslaughter* when he was charged with killing a *woman*."

On December 12, the college's Ciceronian Society, one of two active literary societies on campus, staged a debate on the subject of the trial, still so fresh in the memories of the students. The question resolved was "that from the evidence produced, Watkins ought to have been convicted of murder in the first degree." The actual transcript of the debate does not survive in the Ciceronian minutes, but almost certainly the nature and applicability of circumstantial evidence were key points of argument. The final verdict was much closer than the jury deliberations were. Of the eight judges, five agreed with the positive and three the negative. The *Roanoke Times* noted that "a number of ladies were present, who enjoyed the earnestness of with which the question was debated."

CHARLES WATKINS WAS A dead man walking. But as it would turn out, he would outlive two of the people involved in his drama. On December 9, the *Roanoke Times* and the *Salem Times-Register* reported the death of Mary Coxe, the sister of Fannie Coxe, after a paralyzing stroke suffered just after the trial concluded. Although she did not testify, she was presumably in the cabin when Charles and Susan passed by on the fateful night the previous April.[37]

On the same day, death called at the home of Henry Webber as well. The former deputy turned private detective, the investigator who had doggedly continued the search for Charles Watkins when all trails had grown cold, the man who traveled to North Carolina to see to the extradition, passed away after an unspecified illness. He was only forty-two; it will be recalled that his wife had died in childbirth less than six months before. Webber was also predeceased by a first wife and five of his children, leaving four others orphaned.

Watkins would certainly have heard the news of the untimely death of his adversary. Whether or not he took any satisfaction in the fact cannot now be known.

In PROFOUND WAYS, CHARLES Watkins was a man alone. He had never had any particular defenders or supporters, except the attorneys who represented him professionally. It is likely even they were not convinced of his innocence, although they were duty-bound to take his side and make his arguments.

Family and friends had seemingly abandoned him. When he was brought back to Roanoke in custody, the local press had found a few unnamed individuals who had professed belief in his innocence. But since then, the majority of residents of the Roanoke Valley, black and white, seemed to be wholly convinced of his guilt and in full agreement with the sentence passed on him.

But in the aftermath of his trial, one group came to the side of Charles Watkins with comfort, encouragement and spiritual advice: the local Christian community. It was not a group convinced of his guiltlessness. It was a group concerned with his immortal soul.

In November and December, the newspapers reported several ministerial visits to Watkins's cell and, initially, of his receptivity to them. This was not uncommon, of course. Christians had always felt a calling to minister to the imprisoned. Who could benefit more from spiritual guidance than a guilty inmate? Who is in greater need of grace than a convicted sinner? Who should pause to consider his eternal destiny more urgently than a prisoner under a death sentence? It's not surprising that so many of the visitors who stood outside of Charles's cell had Bibles in their hands.

On November 26, the *Roanoke Times* noted that Pastor Benjamin Fox of Salem's First Baptist Church and a Pastor Johnson of the local African American Methodist church had called on Watkins the day before. They "sang and prayed" with him and "left promising to call again." The paper also noted that Charles "has a grand bass voice and sings well."

Again, on December 9, the paper reported that representatives of the Salvation Army had spent two days praying with and for Charles. The prisoner seemed to be responding to such outreaches. According to what the jailer Hening told the paper, Watkins's "whole

Pastor Benjamin Fox, spiritual advisor to Charles Watkins. *Salem Historical Society and Shiloh Baptist Church.*

attention is taken up with religious matters in the endeavor to save his soul," noting also that he "is looking badly and has lost his appetite and his confident smile."

These ministerial visits continued through the month of December and into January, with Fox especially taking the lead. At first, they seemed to make a profound difference in the prisoner. On December 22, the *Roanoke Times* reported that Watkins had "made a profession of religion" the previous Saturday night and noted "if outward appearances are an index to the condition of his mind and heart, he speaks the truth."

However, the genuineness of Charles's religious fervor would become an issue of controversy in ensuing days.

On December 9, the *Roanoke Times* reported that Charles had "given up all hope for a new trial." But in fact, his attorneys were still pursuing the slim chance of an appeal. The newspaper revealed on the twelfth that, at the end of the trial, Pugh had presented to Judge Griffin three "bills of exception," claiming errors in the court's proceedings that had denied their client a fair trial. Griffin, as required, signed and sealed these exceptions for consideration by another court should one deem an appeal necessary.

Pugh's objections dealt with the circumstantial nature of the case ("the verdict is contrary to the evidence") but also more specifically to questions related to the jury instructions. In essence, during the trial, Pugh had lobbied to have the third jury instruction enjoin the jurors that "the proof must show that a body found is the body of the person for whose murder the prisoner is indicted." That verbiage was changed to the third instruction described earlier, a slightly lower burden of proof, dealing with a standard of "beyond all reasonable doubt" instead of positive, irrefutable proof.

Pugh's strategy was clear. No one, at least in the view of the defense, had proven with irrefutable evidence that the body found in Horner's Branch in April was Susan Watkins. Her corpse had been identified, but only by people who had known her for a couple of days at most, Pugh could claim. How could anyone know with absolute certainty that the deceased was in fact Susan Watkins?

In truth, the proof he demanded did not and could not exist. Implicit in the question is whether anyone can know anything at all in a court of law with absolute certainty. This is precisely why courts use a standard of "beyond a reasonable doubt," rather than "beyond any conceivable doubt." Were it necessary to prove every case to the point that no one could imagine an alternate explanation to facts, few, if any, people could ever be convicted of anything.

Pugh, of course, knew this. He occasionally acted as a prosecutor and understood legal standards better than most. He certainly knew the chances were slim of winning an appeal on such a tenuous thread. But it was still his best chance to get an appeal of Watkins's death sentence.

The paper reported that these exceptions would most likely be considered by Judge Henry Blair of the Roanoke County Circuit Court. Should Blair deign to accept the appeal, arguments would likely not be heard until the April session, meaning a long delay in Watkins's sentence. The paper

Circuit court judge Henry Blair. *Salem Historical Society.*

further opined that "the public will criticize very harshly any attempt made to put the Commonwealth to any further unnecessary expense to save Watkins' neck."

However, nothing came of this appeal. It is unclear if the defense dropped the strategy as untenable or if it did come before Judge Blair and he refused to hear the matter. Either way, that avenue for keeping Charles from the scaffold came to a close.

On December 22, the *Roanoke Times* noted in a short update that Watkins seemed "resigned to his fate." With little more than two weeks to live, he was reported to have given up hope. But had he? With all legal appeals exhausted, could he by some miracle change the cards he'd been dealt?

ON DECEMBER 23, WATKINS sent a message to the *Salem Times-Register* office that he would like to make a statement exclusively to that paper. Thinking that he might be ready to make a full confession, two representatives of the paper, Charles Dice Denit and Frank Webber, rushed to the jail, where Deputy Hening granted access to the prisoner's cell. What they found was entirely different from their expectations. The ensuing story, printed on Christmas Day, told of a "pair of wild-looking eyes [telling] of a diseased mind," instead of the calm demeanor he displayed during the trial. The reporters continued: "It took but a moment to convince us that we stood in the presence of a man crazed by religious excitement."

Instead of a confession, the journalists were subjected to an "incoherent story" delivered by a man with a crazed look and wildly waving hands. Although it seemed little more than a rant, the reporters took careful notes of what he had to say and faithfully recorded lengthy passages for their interested readers:

> *"This is not by my desire, but it is the will of God," Watkins began. "He directs me to do this. Here is what the Lord had led me to do...tell Mr. Frank Webber...this is going to be the greatest excitement in Salem as soon as it is revealed....*
>
> *"The Lord revealed to me to send for Mr. Zirkle [the sheriff] and tell him to come here next Sunday evening at 9 o'clock with his carriage, that Judge Griffin and Maj. Ballard, Mr. and Mrs. Hening, and the two white preachers will go with me down to Mr. Fox's church, where he has fixed up a place on the right hand side of the church; and I want you and all the people to come there and sit on the right hand side, and hear me preach the gospel as a token; all the people will come and hear me, and think I am going to preach about my wife; but there is where they are going to get left; I am going to preach about the dear Lord; and I want you to give your whole paper to my preaching, my hymns and all; and all the people to buy a paper, and those that can't buy a paper you to give them one, to be wrapped up and put away as a token of this word of God I am going to preach. It will be something in this world to know.*
>
> *"When I was on trial, how did I sit? Just like a man who thought he wasn't going to he hung: and people asked me, Charlie, do you think you are going to be hung? I told them I left it with the Lord; if I got clear it would be by and through Him, and after I got sentenced did I cry? No, indeed; I just held on to the Bible Mrs. Hening gave me, and trusted in the Lord.*
>
> *"When I preach my text-is going to be the first verse of 23d Psalm: 'The Lord is my shepherd, I shall not want.' Next, first verse of 25th Psalm, 'Unto thee, O Lord, do I lift up my soul'; and then the first verse of 27th Psalm, and the 47th, 48th, 49th, and 50th verses of the 12th chapter of St. John."*

In summation, the nonplussed reporters noted that "the doomed and wretched creature talks in the above strain all the time, and he is either a monomaniac on the subject of having been called to preach...or he is playing crazy to perfection.

"Which it is, we cannot positively say."

Staff of the *Salem Times-Register*. Frank Webber is third from the left; Charles Denit is third from the right. *Salem Historical Society.*

The question pondered by the paper would be heatedly debated over the next few days. Was the condemned prisoner in the Roanoke County jail insane, or was he "playing crazy?" His fate—and a last chance to escape the hangman's noose—would rest on the answer.

OVER THE NEXT COUPLE of days, Charles continued to rave with what the *Roanoke Times* called "misquoted texts from the Bible and ungrammatical prayers." On Christmas Eve, he called for Commonwealth's Attorney Ballard and subjected him to a similar diatribe. It was reported that he'd also asked for Ben Wright to visit him, but it is unknown if that meeting ever took place.

Soon word spread through the town, and spectators began to gather on the sidewalk below his cell window to witness the spectacle and for some to observe the "smart dodge he is playing."

On Christmas Day, attorneys Pugh and Moffett visited Charles in the jail, bringing him a gift of some delicacies to enjoy. But more importantly, they brought with them no fewer than three physicians to evaluate his mental condition: Drs. Oscar Wiley, Joseph J. Shanks and Jacob P. Killian. Shanks and Killian served (with Dr. Baird) on Salem's Board of Health,[38] and Killian had assisted the coroner's jury eight months before. They administered some sort of sedative to the excitable prisoner but would not publicly render any opinion as to his mental state.

The *Roanoke Times* speculated on December 26 about this development with the headline "Is Watkins Crazy? Or Is He Playing Off to Save His Neck?" The reporter opined that this was a strategy to escape the noose and that it would in all likelihood work: "Charles Watkins will probably never be hanged, for with the smartness that has all along characterized his behavior, he has in the last few days developed into a raving lunatic…there is hardly a thinking man in the community but who would be willing to bet that he will ultimately escape the gallows, which he so richly deserves."

That same day, Pugh officially requested before the county court that a "lunacy commission" be appointed by the judge to evaluate the mental health of the condemned man. Commonwealth's Attorney Ballard, surprisingly, did not object—perhaps his visit with Charles earlier in the week had created some concerns in his own mind. Judge Griffin replied that he would personally consult with some physicians and follow their recommendation as to the need for such a commission.

Griffin did indeed ask three local physicians to act as the commission to gauge Watkins's mental health. Drs. Shanks and Killian, who had visited with the two attorneys, were joined by Dr. W.D. Armstrong, a local doctor/pharmacist (and former mayor of Salem) who frequently treated inmates at the jail. Armstrong, in fact, had visited Watkins every day since this bout of erratic behavior had started, often administering a sedative.

Shanks, having served in a lunatic asylum before, was described as something of an expert on the treatment of the insane, to the extent that such a thing existed in 1891 by modern standards. The *Roanoke Times* also hinted that he was personally opposed to capital punishment.

On December 31, the three physicians visited Watkins to interview him. The reporter for the *Roanoke Times* tried to insinuate himself into the proceedings but was unceremoniously banished from the jail. Undeterred, he parked himself on the street beneath Watkins's cell window but could hear none of the questions and only snatches of the prisoner's "well-feigned ravings." Part of what was overheard was the proclamation that Charles was "Jesus Christ….My father has sent me here to awaken you to your condition." He also seemingly threatened to kill "all of the Negroes in town." The reporter remained convinced that it was all an act.

The three men returned for at least two days to evaluate Charles, and on January 2, they delivered to Judge Griffin their conclusion. Charles Watkins was not insane. Whether this was a medical diagnosis—that his mental state was clinically normal—or a legal one—that whatever mental defect he may display was insufficient to halt his execution—is unclear. But the result was the same either way. Charles Watkins would hang for the murder of his wife on January 8. The last path to avoid the noose was closed.

So, was Charles Watkins insane in December 1891? Or was he indeed faking lunacy to escape his sentence?

There is, of course, no way to diagnose the psychological state of a man who has been dead for more than a century. Few, if any, people at the time seemed convinced of the authenticity of his erratic behavior. The newspapers were decidedly opposed to his receiving any clemency and published several bits of anecdotal evidence that it was all, indeed, a sham.

One morning, a jailhouse attendant brought Charles his breakfast and was greeted with the usual vicious diatribe. Sheriff Zirkle happened to be in the jail at the time and told the attendant to leave the tray outside of his cell. As soon as everyone was out of earshot, Charles quietly ate his breakfast.

A fellow inmate, Farrar Frog, locked up for assaulting a police officer, reported that Charles was always "perfectly quiet" when the corridors were empty, but when he heard footsteps or voices approaching he launched into his noisy prayers and songs.

Even Dr. Shanks, the resident expert on the mad, expressed professional skepticism to the press. In his experience, he said, the truly insane did not make claims to be Jesus Christ. Only a person deliberately hoping to be taken for insane by offending as many people as he could ever committed such blasphemous pretense.

But on the other hand, some of Charles's behavior would seem to indicate an unbalanced psyche. For instance, as will be seen, his ravings did not end when the commission declared him sane. They continued up to his very last words, when he had nothing to gain from shamming insanity. It might also be noted that had he been found insane, he may have escaped the gallows, but he would not have been freed. He would have spent the rest of his life in a mental institution—not facilities noted for their pleasant atmosphere in nineteenth-century America. Feigning insanity was hardly a sane choice.

It certainly seems in the realm of possibility that Charles Watkins was mentally unbalanced in his final weeks. He was a man under enormous mental stress, after all. His entire adult life, he had exuded a cool and collected demeanor. Popular, urbane, charming, he was used to getting his way. He had always found his way out of trouble and had escaped the law on more than one occasion. But now he was not only in custody but also on death row. For a man at least a little narcissistic, it may well have been enough to unhinge his mind.

Perhaps the two binary choices—either insanity or faking to avoid the gallows—were not actually mutually exclusive.

But in the end, it was a false lead, a nonstarter from the beginning as a legal strategy. There were certainly legal provisions and abundant precedent to mandate that a mentally diseased defendant need not be held responsible for his crimes. One important standard was (and is) whether the accused could tell the difference between right and wrong in terms of his wrongdoing.

But, as the *Roanoke Times* had pointed out on December 27, nothing in the law prevented the hanging of a man who was found to have become insane *after* his crime and *after* his trial. The insanity defense dealt with the mental state of the defendant *when the crime was committed*, not after he'd been found guilty.

No evidence of insanity had been introduced in the courtroom. Watkins's attorneys had never suggested he was incapable of knowing that murder was morally wrong. Indeed, his months-long effort to evade arrest would have immediately suggested otherwise and rendered such an argument moot.

Watkins may well have died an insane man. But he had killed his wife and stood trial for the crime with his mental faculties intact. That was the deciding factor.

There was nothing more to be done on behalf of the condemned man, except wait for the preordained date of his death.

A JUDICIAL HANGING IN Roanoke County continued to capture the public imagination—and consequently sell newspapers. No one had seen gallows in the county in eleven years, resulting in something of a morbid fascination with the machinery of death among the public—or at least the writers of the *Roanoke Times*. As a result, a minute description survives.

Early on, there was some speculation that Roanoke County would buy the gallows used recently by Botetourt to hang Henry Nowlin. The authorities in Fincastle had kept the structure intact in hopes of just such a transaction. But instead, Sheriff Zirkle contracted with John Parrish and Sons to build the scaffold and the required fence around the site. Thomas Snead was the lead carpenter for the job. Work began soon after Christmas. Construction was mere feet from the jail, meaning Watkins could hear the sound of hammers and saws.

When completed, the scaffold measured eight and a half feet high, the top reached by a flight of twelve steps. A railing surrounded the platform, with a three-by-four-foot trapdoor in the center. The trap would be opened by two spring hinges, but for reasons not entirely clear they would be sprung not by a lever atop the platform but from inside the courthouse. A cord ran through a series of pulleys and into a window where an operator would await the signal.

A rumor had circulated in December that the same rope used to hang Marcus Hawley in 1880 would be reused in this case. But Sheriff Zirkle obtained a rope in Richmond (where he traveled in late December to deliver another prisoner to the state prison). There, an expert, who desired anonymity, tied the hangman's knot for him. Returning to Salem, Zirkle locked the rope in a safe.

Once upon a time in Virginia hangings had been done in public, in open view of any spectators who desired to watch (and, as a rule, many did). More recent state law mandated that hangings be carried out in a fenced enclosure, ideally adjacent to the jail, out of public view. Snead therefore constructed a fence enclosing a space of only sixteen by twenty-six feet, but it reached some twenty feet high. Some spectators would be allowed inside, but the fence around the jail yard would be too high for anyone outside to witness the deed. Zirkle would tightly control access—even printing tickets.

No detail was overlooked in preparing for this unpleasant occasion. By early January, all was ready.

Except the prisoner.

THE FAILURE OF THE ploy to use insanity to escape his sentence—if that is what it was—did not mean Charles returned to his previous genial self. In fact, the *Roanoke Times* opined that "realizing that the crazy business has played out, [he's] becoming desperate and ugly." On January 4, Dr. Armstrong called to check on his patient, who was brought out of his cell for examination. When it was time to be returned, Watkins defiantly refused, grabbing onto the outside of his bars in an attempt to stay free. He called to another prisoner to come to his aid as he had promised, which the *Times* reporter took as evidence that Watkins had tried to hatch an escape plan. It took five men—including town officials who happened to be in the jail on another matter—to return the prisoner to his cell.

The tussle convinced Sheriff Zirkle to appoint a "death watch" for Watkins—men to stay with him and be sure he did not harm himself.

Samuel Strickler and John Rhodes were appointed to this task; Strickler had stood guard over Susan Watkins's body on the night after the murder nine months before.

On the sixth, Dr. Armstrong called again, and brought with him two black pastors (unnamed by the *Roanoke Times*, but likely one was Benjamin Fox). But Watkins was "so insulting to them that they left in disgust."

However, by that evening, Charles seemed to have calmed down somewhat. On Thursday, the last full day he had to live, the condemned man was quieter, eating and sleeping well. Dr. Armstrong spent the occasion of his final official visit to try, for ninety minutes, to convince Watkins to make a final confession. But the only answer was resignation: "My sins are blotted out. If my Father says I must hang it is all right."

Nevertheless, before Armstrong left, Charles asked him to ask Pastor Fox to visit, which he did in the evening. Fox also seemed to encourage a full confession, for the spiritual benefits of dying with a clean conscience. Pugh and Moffett also dropped by, but not wanting to interrupt this time with a religious advisor, they departed quietly.

There was a good deal of speculation about whether Charles would issue a confession and a good deal of encouragement for him to do so. Such jailhouse confessionals before an execution were seemingly obligatory in those days, a way to not only come clean but also warn others to avoid the same sad fate. Nowlin had made just such a confession before he was hanged in November. Farrar Frog, the prisoner in an adjacent cell, told a reporter that Charles spoke to him several times about the crime and his reasons for it; however, the reporter did not seem to give much credence to Frog's account, thinking he sought notoriety.

Watkins had, of course, as good as confessed to the murder of his wife in his letter to Ben Wright months before. But that admission of guilt contained little in the way of satisfying detail for those who craved a deathbed confession. Would the convicted murder come clean before the noose closed around his neck?

FRIDAY, JANUARY 8, 1892, dawned cold and clear in Salem. Snow had fallen earlier in the week, allowing the popular bachelor Robert "Country Bob" Logan to break out his horse-drawn sleigh and offer rides, to the delight of local children. It is likely snow was still visible in places. But the weather was no deterrent to the crowd that began to mill about the courthouse and jail hours before the scheduled time. Only a handful would be allowed into the compound to see the actual hanging. The rest would congregate outside of the twenty-foot fence with macabre fascination. The *Roanoke Times* would note that "there was nobody in the crowd who disagreed with the jury that convicted Watkins, and they soon became impatient."

About 9:30 a.m., Sergeant Jacob Brugh Frier, the constable for the town of Salem, stationed a team of twelve guards around the neighborhood of the courthouse. While there didn't seem to be any specific reason to expect unrest, Frier apparently thought it prudent to take precautions.

Some of the people milling about in expectancy almost certainly were reading the morning edition of the *Roanoke Times*. Of course, the paper had gone to print the night before, so no details of the hanging could have been published. The summary headline proclaimed "Watkins' Death Trap Ready—A Sensational Hanging Expected—Watkins Desperate and May Make Trouble—The Trap Completed Yesterday and Thoroughly Tested—The Drop to Fall About Eleven o'Clock This Morning—A New Manilla Rope to Do the Work."

Soon after the hanging, the *Roanoke Times* would issue an extra with the details of the proceedings and later brag that its journalism was "Equal to the Occasion." Word of the completed hanging reached Roanoke from Salem by telegraph at 12:14 p.m. The extra was on the press by 12:25 p.m., and by 12:30, copies were on the street. Over 1,400 extras were printed, and "the town absorbed them as a sponge takes up water."

DESPITE THE EXPECTATION THAT he might make trouble, Charles Watkins arose early in the morning and appeared quite calm. Having refused a new set of clothes offered by the jailer, Charles dressed in an older suit from his trunk, which he'd had since before his arrest. The dark suit, shirt and collar were reported to be "somewhat soiled." With uncut hair and a longer, unkempt beard, Watkins bore little resemblance to the "same neat and dudish head waiter of time gone by." That carefree man, so particular about his appearance, so ready to charm customers and woo women, was already gone.

About 9:00 a.m., Hening brought Charles his last meal. Watkins had expressed no preference for the menu, so Hening had arranged with Fred Webber, a cook at the Southern Hotel in Roanoke, to prepare something (why he sent all the way to Roanoke instead of one of the Salem hotels is unclear). Webber appeared with a huge repast: oatmeal and cream, tenderloin steak, broiled oysters (Watkins was fond of seafood), poached eggs on toast, potatoes, coffee and a glass of wine for the condemned. Charles "ate ravenously" and complimented Webber on the meal.

Sometime before 10:00 a.m., one of Watkins's attorneys, Marshall McClung, came to see him, but whether by chance or appointment is not clear. Soon after, McClung was joined by Reverend Fox, who had been requested by Charles. The two men spoke with Charles and encouraged his cooperation with the authorities. They also received from him what the authorities, the press and the public seemed to expect: a full confession.

CHARLES'S LAST-MINUTE CONFESSION IS of obvious interest, but it raises some questions for the historian. The only record of it is the account by a *Roanoke Times* reporter on January 9.[39] He was outside of the cell but at some distance—the writer acknowledges that he could not hear the conversation fully. On the one hand, Watkins had nothing to lose by telling his story at that point; on the other, it must be kept in mind that he had been showing at least some evidence of mental disturbance in the weeks prior. It should also be kept in mind that the newspaper had every reason to embellish and sensationalize the account in order to sell papers. Nonetheless, the confession fairly accurately tracked the known facts of the murder, and there is no obvious reason to dismiss the basic details of his account.

Charles revealed that he first determined "to get rid" of his wife in the summer of 1890, when he abandoned her for Ida Friebel. But since they quickly put half a continent between themselves and Susan, it was not until the Sunday night that she arrived unexpectedly in Roanoke that he finally determined to kill his wife.

Nothing in his confession indicates he wrote to Susan to lure her to Virginia; nothing indicates that Edith was complicit in the planning of the crime. But neither did anything he said necessarily rule out these things.

On the night before the murder, Charles stated that after leaving the Coxe cabin with the borrowed lantern, Susan protested that she would go no further and wanted to return to Roanoke. The two quarreled, and Charles pulled his gun, shooting at her three or four times and hitting her twice. He then said he struck her in the head with either a rock or the gun. He left her for dead, leaving the revolver there on the ground.

Proceeding on to the cabin of Taylor Watkins, he told his uncle that he had killed Susan, but in self-defense. Soon, however, Susan arrived at the cabin bleeding from her neck and wrist. Her pleas for a doctor were ignored.

In his description of the crime, Charles noted that Ben Wright had no prior awareness whatsoever of the murder, but repeatedly incriminated Taylor and Lucy Watkins in concealing details of that night, especially the shooting.

The next morning, Charles admitted that he left with Susan to have her wounds treated by Dr. Dillard, but after arriving at a secluded spot, he suddenly "took up a rock and knocked her in the head." He rolled her lifeless body off of the path and into the creek, leaving the blood-stained rock there, and returned to his uncle's cabin. The next morning, he left for Roanoke with Ida, who had been secreted in the cabin the whole night.

Perhaps this confession, such as it was, was less earth-shaking in its revelations than the press hoped. Little had been revealed that was not already known. However, Charles did reveal some previously unknown details about his departure from Gum Spring with Edith Friebel, details that will be recounted presently.

A rumor began to circulate around town that Watkins had admitted to other murders in his confession, but McClung would deny this in the press the next day.

By the time Charles finished his version of events the previous April, it was approaching 11:00 a.m. Sheriff Zirkle appeared in the corridor with Hening and some other assistants, signaling that the time had come. McClung reached through the bars and shook Charles's hand, telling him to be brave. If Pugh or Moffett were in attendance that morning, there is no record of it.

Dr. Armstrong came to the cell and asked if the prisoner knew him. Charles replied that he did and always had recognized him. Armstrong asked then why he "had acted so strangely" in previous days. Charles answered rather nonsensically: he "thought on Christmas Day he had gotten genuine religion, but was mistaken." He also stated that "some kind of gas" had gotten into his cell and addled his mind.

Fox then stepped forward, perhaps prompted by Zirkle, and asked if he were ready to go. Charles responded defiantly: "I am not afraid to die. I feel that there is no fire, nor nothing to burn me. Jesus is with me and we will see whether anyone can hang me or not." But he also asked Fox to follow him to the scaffold and pray for him.

The cell was unlocked and Charles brought into the passageway. Hening began to put handcuffs on him, but Watkins protested. Fox immediately chastised him, telling him to "submit to the law." The prisoner obeyed, and his arms were cuffed and pinioned to his front. A black cap was placed on his head, but the veil was not lowered, allowing Charles to see to walk.

There was one last requirement. Sheriff Zirkle read aloud the death warrant, making the subsequent events legally appropriate. Jailer Hening and another unnamed deputy then each took an arm and began walking Charles out of the jail to his fate.

Charles walked through the building confidently, but when he exited into the yard, he faltered a bit. A large crowd was in the enclosure, men who had been granted tickets to the event and allowed to enter through the tightly guarded treasurer's office. A duly appointed jury of twelve men was included, tasked with being certain that the proceedings were carried out properly and legally. Ballard was there, as were Drs. Armstrong, Baird, Shanks, Killian and Saunders, all of whom had had contact with the case. There were reporters for various papers and some twenty men like John Thomason who had been offered tickets by the sheriff. There is no record of any of the Watkins family being in attendance.

But it did not seem to be the sight of the crowd that caused Watkins to hesitate. It was the sight of the gallows. The two guards at his arms pulled him forward and helped him ascend the twelve steep steps to the gallows.

Atop the platform, Fox took Watkins's shackled hands as he was guided to the center of the trap door. Zirkle asked Watkins if he had anything to say. Competing versions of Watkins's last words exist. The *Roanoke Times*, in the January 8 extra, gave this version: "There is no man in this world, or in the world to come, can hang me. I am so glad that Jesus is my Saviour. Jesus, see the condition I am in!" Turning to the guard holding the noose, he cried, "Don't choke me!" Finally, he shouted hysterically, "I am the son of Jesus Christ!"

The *Salem Times-Register* recounted the following: "There is no man on earth who can hang me! I am the son of Jesus Christ and all the men in the world can't hang me!"

Meanwhile, a competing and short-lived paper, the *Salem Saturday Sun*, had Watkins shrieking this three or four times: "There is no man in this world who can hang me!" Finally, he cried, "I am the son of Jesus Christ and all the men in the world can't hang me!"[40]

Whichever version is correct, it seems that Charles's frenetic religious outcries continued to the very last, perhaps final evidence that, as the *Roanoke Times* guessed, "brooding over his impending fate…[had] unbalanced his mind."

The *Sun* version further has Zirkle cutting Watkins off: "If you have a warning to offer, say it. We haven't time for a sermon." The other papers did not report this, but Charles fell silent.

On January 8, the *Roanoke Times* reported that Pastor Fox began a prayer but was "rudely and roughly repulsed" by Watkins. But the next day, the paper noted that Fox offered a short but impressive prayer "in which he implored the divine mercy for the soul of the condemned man." The two Salem papers agreed that Fox had the opportunity to pray for Charles.

With that, the prisoner's legs were fastened together by straps at the knees and ankles, and the noose was placed around his neck. Hening lowered the veil over his face, taking a moment to shake the hand of the prisoner he had guarded faithfully since July, and say good-bye.

Zirkle pulled a handkerchief from his pocket to use as the signal for the man in the courthouse who actually controlled the trapdoor—his own son Mack Zirkle. At 11:17 a.m., he waved the handkerchief, and the younger Zirkle sharply pulled the cord. The trap opened, and Charles Watkins, condemned wife murderer, fell into eternity.

Soon afterward, the somber crowd both within and without the fenced enclosure began to disperse. Reporters rushed to the telegraph office to report the news, while the physicians lingered to certify that the death sentence had indeed been carried out. Charles's neck had snapped instantly, as expected. After six minutes, Dr. Armstrong felt for a pulse and found none; after half an hour, the body was cut down and examined. Charles Watkins was officially pronounced dead.

Soon after this, members of Charles's family arrived with a coffin and claimed the remains. The paper did not bother to record exactly who it was, but likely Taylor and Lucy Watkins, perhaps Addie Anderson, maybe even Ben and Mary Wright, came to do right by the body of their relative, a relative who had gone so wrong.

The family returned home and buried Charles Watkins on Brush Mountain, perhaps in the graveyard now known as Gum Spring Cemetery. Long forgotten and neglected, there is only one gravestone there today, for an Obadiah Akers who died in 1905. But at least forty-three others are buried there without any marker, and oral tradition places members of the Watkins family in some of the unmarked graves.[41] If this was indeed the final resting place of the last man to be judicially hanged in Roanoke County, the exact spot was soon forgotten, just as so much of his story would soon fade into the mists of history.

WHERE WAS IDA?

On April 9, 1892, the *Roanoke Times* ran a two-sentence retrospective under a column titled "Brevities": "Thursday, April 7th inst., was the anniversary of the killing of Susan Watkins by Charles Watkins, who was hanged last January. Justice was swift and sure in his case."

As noted before, some may have quibbled with the swiftness of the case, spanning the better part of a year from crime to punishment, given the customary few weeks for court trials of those days. Nonetheless, the surety of justice could not be denied, and no one at the time seemed to find any fault in the ultimate verdict. A man had killed his wife, all evidence pointed to his guilt and he received the recompense for the crime as defined by law of the day. To be sure, the story of Susan and Charles Watkins would play out somewhat differently—and more slowly—if it occurred today. But by the standards of 1891, the trial was almost a textbook case of how justice could be satisfied.

In a society marked by endemic racism, a black man received a fair trial, with the rights of the accused respected and protected. He had some of the best attorneys in the region defending him; he received multiple continuances in the trial to prepare a case; he was able to appeal the verdict, albeit unsuccessfully; when his mental stability came into question, his attorneys were able to ask the court for due consideration.

Charles Watkins was found guilty and executed for his crime, and it was for a single reason: his guilt had been proven in a court of law by abundant evidence.

Interestingly, the hanging of Charles Watkins did not end all discussion of the case. On January 21, 1892, the *Roanoke Times* published a small story in a tongue-in-cheek style reporting on various sightings of "Watkins' Ghost."

The article quipped that after his hanging, "It was very naturally supposed that [Watkins] would cease to be a disturbing element in this latitude. But not so. Although Charles' life was forfeited and his body coffined…there are numerous people with whom he seems to be present too frequently for their peace of mind." The story went on to tell of a member of the paper's staff whose sleep had been repeatedly interrupted by visions of Watkins shrieking, "You can't hang me!" It was also claimed that other members of the press who covered the hanging had seen similar apparitions, and Ed Oppenheimer, who had sold Charles a pint of whiskey the night after the murder and who also attended the hanging, had also seen the departed murderer.

Another, if less spectral anecdote, involved Fred Webber, the hotel cook who had prepared Watkins's last meal. He claimed to be bothered by an idle hotel worker, who bore a strong resemblance to Charles Watkins, loitering around his Southern Hotel in Roanoke, seemingly taking enjoyment from disturbing patrons.

A few days after, the paper revisited the issue of Watkins ghost with the same tongue-in-cheek sense. It suggested that those who saw the apparitions could benefit from the Keeley Institute, a new treatment center in Salem for alcoholism.

The ghost stories were, of course, hardly credible. But they suggested something worthy of notice: the trial and execution of Charles Watkins had made a pronounced impact on the community. In a county where death sentences were rare occurrences, this one invariably left an impression.

AND YET THE STORY of Charles Watkins's crime and punishment soon faded from public memory in the Roanoke Valley. A murder and subsequent trial that had captivated the public and dominated headlines locally—and made the papers across the nation—was soon for all practical purposes forgotten.

The *Salem Times-Register* would decades later look back on the Watkins affair on three occasions. In February 1937, it printed some recollections of the hanging from aged residents John Thomason and Watts Dillard; much of the same information was again published in May 1938 in a massive historical edition of the paper for Roanoke County's centennial. Then for Salem's sesquicentennial in 1952, a smaller historical tabloid gave the hanging a few column inches. These stories concentrated on the hanging itself, the last hour of Charles's life, with the rest of the drama abridged to a summary of only a few sentences.

Local history surveys have universally overlooked the case. William McCauley's massive *History of Roanoke County* (1902) makes no mention of it, even though McCauley was clerk of court in 1891 and sat through the trial. George Jack's shorter 1912 history also ignores the case, as does a 1940 WPA history of the valley. Histories of Roanoke City by Raymond Barnes (1968, troubling) and Clare White (1982, wonderful), Norwood Middleton's excellent *Salem: A Virginia Chronicle* (1986), Deedie Kagey's sesquicentennial history of the county *When Past Is Prologue* (1988), Reginald Shareef's *The Roanoke Valley's African American History* (1996), Rand Dotson's more recent *Roanoke, Virginia 1882–1912: Magic City of the New South* (2007)—in none of these seminal sources for the history of the region will you find the names of Susan or Charles Watkins.

Why? What accounts for the historical amnesia submerging the Watkins case? There are many answers. Neither Charles nor Susan had children to carry on their legacies. Susan had no family or longtime friends anywhere near Virginia to pass on her story; Charles's extended family had no reason to draw attention to the sad end of a wayward relative—and every reason to allow the episode to fade from memory.

Further, the story would also seem to have been, in the minds of almost everyone, an open-and-shut case. No one came forward to defend Charles or to challenge the death sentence—by all indications, the verdict was accepted by all. There was no one to turn the Watkins case into a cause célèbre, a rallying cry against injustice. Nor was there reason to do so.

Neither was the case one to which the community as a whole would be apt to draw attention. Local boy kills his wife, goes to the gallows—this is not the sort of story on which civic boosterism is built. No one tried to cover up the history of the Watkins murder. But as a rule, no one saw a reason to keep talking about it. The Watkins affair was merely pushed so far back into memory that it eventually disappeared from public recollection.

But that's not to say it was insignificant. The execution of Charles Watkins was the last judicial hanging in Roanoke County—in fact, the last application of the death sentence by any means. By 1908, Virginia had opened a state penitentiary in Richmond and mandated that all capital punishments in the Commonwealth be performed there.[42] By 1909, the new technology of the electric chair had replaced the noose as the method of executions.

THE LEGAL AUTHORITIES INVOLVED in the case remained prominent citizens for years to come. Sheriff George W. Zirkle remained in office until 1908, when he returned to farming for his final years. He lived until 1915. M.G. McClung, the junior member of the defense team, continued a rewarding and respected legal practice the rest of his days, dying in 1932.

William Ballard, the prosecutor, served only one term as Commonwealth's Attorney for Roanoke County, stepping aside in 1895. He then went into private practice and achieved great success: "Major Ballard is in command of a lucrative law practice and enjoys the confidence, respect, and esteem of all who know him,"[43] bragged a biography in 1912. No doubt he looked back on his courtroom success in the Watkins case as the highlight of his time as prosecutor. Ballard died in 1920.

Arthur Benton Pugh's career took him in different directions after the trial. Apparently, the mountainous climate of Roanoke County did not agree with him and his family. In February 1896, he and his wife lost their young son Benton; soon after this he accepted a position in Washington, D.C., with the Department of the Interior, the job he had held before coming to Salem. In August of that year, a daughter was born to the couple, but perhaps the pregnancy wrecked the health of his wife, Louise. She died in November.

Pugh remained in D.C. with the department and served for a while as a special assistant to the attorney general handling land fraud cases.[44] In December 1916, he passed away and was returned to Salem to be buried next to his wife.

Judge Wingfield Griffin served only two more years as judge for the county court, resigning in 1893. Oddly, he then accepted the lower position of clerk for the court over which he had presided for years. He resigned from that position in 1898 to take command of the local militia unit, the Jeff Davis Rifles, as they prepared to go to Cuba to serve in the Spanish-American War. Griffin and his men never made it out of Florida, but they proudly were ready to go. It would often be remarked of Griffin afterward that the boy who wore the gray in the Civil War would proudly wear the blue of the United States as a man.

After the war, Griffin returned to Salem and engaged in business, especially iron mining concerns in the region.[45] Griffin died in 1930 at age eighty-three, one of Salem's last Confederate veterans, beloved by his neighbors.

William Moffett's career as a private attorney came to an end in 1893 when he was appointed judge of the county court as Griffin's successor. He held that position on the bench until 1902, when under a new state constitution,

Judge Wingfield Griffin in his older years. *Salem Historical Society.*

the old county court system was abolished. In 1906, however, the legislature appointed Moffett as judge of the Twentieth Judicial Circuit of Virginia, and he again donned black robes.[46]

Moffett is probably best remembered for sparking a 1910 tempest over academic freedom at Roanoke College, where he was on the board of trustees. Home sick one day from court, he chanced to pick up a textbook used in a history class at the school and found it entirely insulting to the memory of the Confederacy and the heroes of the "Lost Cause" he revered. Others found the text, Henry Elson's *History of United States*, to be a balanced treatment of the war.

Moffett demanded the textbook be banned on campus and the trustees be allowed to monitor classroom content for suitability; the school president refused to compromise his faculty's academic freedom. Moffett soon led an exodus of trustees, resigning from the board and vocally criticizing the school. The divisive episode garnered national attention and lost the college many southern supporters in the short term. Today, the college is widely admired for its difficult stand, and Moffett is usually, and understandably, castigated. But forgotten is the time that Moffett gave all of his considerable legal acumen in a futile attempt to keep a black man from the gallows. William Walter Moffett died in 1926.

ARGUABLY, THE WATKINS CASE can stand as evidence that the deplorable race relations of nineteenth-century Virginia did not always have to mean miscarriages of justice. But it certainly doesn't prove that the Roanoke Valley was somehow exempt from racism or racial violence.

What was avoided in the Charles Watkins case, if it was ever even truly a threat, became shockingly evident in Roanoke City over the next two years. Two African American men accused of crimes were savagely lynched in ugly scenes of violence, and a third was nearly subjected to such extralegal punishment.

The day after Watkins was hanged, the local papers announced that police officer Tom Mabry had died. The month before, he had been struck in the head while arresting a suspect; one Jeff Dooley, a black man with a criminal past, was identified as the assailant. He was arrested, and when word spread that he was in the jail, threats of a lynching began to rumble through the city. Such a thing was narrowly averted when Dooley was quickly spirited out of town. After Mabry's death, Dooley was tried for murder and sentenced to death, but he died of consumption in jail before the sentence could be carried out.

Even more troubling was the case of William Lavender. In February 1892, two young girls reported being attacked by a black man wearing rubber boots. While several men matching such a vague description were suspected, attention soon fell on Lavender. The girls identified him as the assailant, although their certainty could surely be questioned in retrospect.

Lavender was arrested and taken to jail; when his location became known, a mob gathered to seize him. The suspect was moved to another location, but the secret quickly leaked out and the mob found him. Lavender was hanged soon afterward; he confessed to, at most, bumping into one of the girls while intoxicated—but this confession was made while a noose was already around his neck. Sadly, the local press and many prominent citizens seemed to endorse the unlawful violence.

These episodes pale in comparison to Roanoke's lynch riot of 1893. In September of that year, a white woman named Sallie Bishop was attacked and robbed by a black assailant. Soon, a Thomas Smith had been arrested, although his only connection to the crime may have been wearing a hat like the one Mrs. Bishop had described.

That afternoon, a belligerent crowd of between one and two thousand, many intoxicated, gathered outside of the Roanoke jail. Much of the crowd seemed to be under the mistaken opinion that Bishop had been raped or even murdered, and they demanded the prisoner be released to them. The authorities were determined to keep Smith in custody and put him on trial. Mayor Henry Trout called out the local militia to protect the jail.

Later that evening, the crowd, having grown to a reputed five thousand angry demonstrators, stormed the jail despite the infantrymen guarding it. Shots rang out, although who initiated the firefight will never be known. By the end of the melee, eight men were dead and more than thirty wounded, including Mayor Trout, who was spirited out of town for his safety.

Smith was initially removed from the jail for safekeeping, but the next day, police officers decided to return him to the jail. The mob was still active and learned of his whereabouts (perhaps tipped off by the police themselves). They found Smith and wrested him away from the officers. Not long afterward, he was hanging from a hickory limb, having maintained his innocence to the end. Members of the ghoulish mob were so proud of their actions that they cut off pieces of Smith's clothing, and even his ears, as souvenirs.[47]

Local historian Clare White would later claim that the 1893 lynch riot was "not only closed, it was buried, weighed down with a stone of shame. Rarely was it ever mentioned again."[48] In recent decades, the event has deservedly gotten much more attention and analysis because of what it says about the state of race relations in Virginia at the time. (White's description, however, fairly accurately describes the Watkins case.)

Salem and rural Roanoke County were, of course, smaller, more congenial places than the boisterous metropolis of Roanoke City, and hence less prone to the violent eruptions seen in 1892–93. But the relative calm with which the community handled the Watkins episode makes an interesting comparison nonetheless.

BY AND LARGE, THE court got it right in the Watkins trial. But there is one particular instance where justice seemed a little too blind: in uncovering the role in the murder of Edith "Ida" Friebel.

As previously discussed, when Friebel was released from jail, she hopped the first available train and disappeared from the remainder of the story in Virginia. The trial postponements, granted to allow Charles's attorneys to bring in out-of-state witnesses, may hint at some effort to locate and question Edith, but if so, they were fruitless. She never returned to the Roanoke Valley and never answered in court for her role, if any, in the murder.

There is no way to track Ida's movements after hopping that westbound train in the spring of 1891. Did she return to her parents' house? Did she go back to Milwaukee or Chicago and submerge herself in urban anonymity? Did she change her name to avoid detection? Was she constantly looking over her shoulder for months? Or did she resolutely close that chapter in her life and move on the next, never looking back at all?

More compelling questions should be asked: Did she get away with murder while her lover and accomplice went to the gallows? Or was she entirely innocent in the affair, as she claimed while in custody?

Of course, we can't answer any of these questions with any certitude. But there are intriguing hints that the role of Ida Friebel in the murder of Susan Watkins was more than that of innocent bystander. To be sure, by all accounts and according to all evidence, Charles alone dealt the fatal blows that ended the life of his wife. But it will be recalled that the coroner's jury immediately after the crime named Edith as an accessory to the murder, either before or after the fact.

It will also be recalled that on the night that Susan appeared at the Washingtons' boardinghouse to confront her husband, Charles and Ida are both known to have gone to the Hotel Felix. Did they confer there on what to do? Did they even conspire? We can only guess. The two were also seen whispering in the back room of Taylor Watkins's cabin not long before Susan left with Charles to meet her doom.

Perhaps most intriguing is part of the confession Charles made on the morning of his death. Recall for a moment that not long after his return to Salem in custody, Charles spoke to a reporter and unexpectedly asked him if any money had been found on Susan's body. He seemed genuinely curious and surprised when the answer was no. It is also worth remembering that Ida had enough money while in the Roanoke jail to hire an attorney and then to buy a ticket away from Roanoke. (She had received a check from her father, but her resources seemed to exceed even that gift.)

Then, months later in his last hours alive, Charles told his attorney M.G. McClung, Pastor Fox and the eavesdropping reporter a detail about the day of the murder that no one else could have known. He confessed that (as reported in third person by the *Roanoke Times* on January 9):

> *Soon after this he started with Edith for Roanoke, stopping at the little branch to see if Susan was dead. And there Edith took out of the right stocking of the murdered woman a pocket book, and seeing Susan was dead they went on. Charles said that Susan had seventy-five dollars on her person, but he did not take it.*

Of course, this confession, recorded secondhand in the newspaper and coming from a man who may have become mentally unstable, proves nothing. But it is entirely plausible, and Charles had no reason to lie about it. If true, it means that Ida Friebel would have been abundantly aware that a crime of violence had been committed against her rival. Since she inspected the body for signs of life and found none, murder could have been the only conclusion. She had to have known that Charles perpetrated the act. And then she physically handled the body and allegedly removed from it a large sum of money.

Perhaps the assertion by the condemned man was untrue; we can't know. But if it were an accurate statement of events, it would make Edith at least a material witness to a homicide and possibly much more culpable than some believed her to be. She could hardly then have been the innocent, regretful girl the local press at first assumed her to be ("deserted by her kinsfolk, estranged from her church, she knows not what may happen next and in her unhappy, wretched and friendless condition she prays for death…she had no knowledge of the crime, nor was she an accessory by word or deed…").

Conceivably, Edith Friebel was even more blameworthy. Perhaps she cajoled her lover to kill his wife so that the two could finally be together. Or perhaps she knew nothing about it until she saw the body in the creek. We can never know, since she was never brought to court and compelled under oath to tell the truth, the whole truth and nothing but the truth.

But if Charles spoke the truth in his confession, Edith Friebel may have indeed gotten away with murder, or at least some part in it.

So WHAT BECAME OF Ida Friebel alias Edith Friebel alias Ida Watkins?

Once again, it's impossible to discover where she might have spent the weeks and months immediately after leaving Roanoke, but she does reappear in the historical record. By 1900, according to the census of that year in the city of Chicago, Edith was employed as a book canvasser, apparently selling books door-to-door. She was living in a boardinghouse in Ward 1 operated by one Peter Bateman, a French Canadian tailor.

In 1901, Edith and Peter were married, despite his being seventeen years her senior. The wedding was on June 25 at Holy Angel's Church in Chicago. Soon they had a son, Edwin. If his age of nine recorded in the 1910 census is correct, he was born by the end of 1901, and she may well have been pregnant at the wedding.

By 1920, the family was living in Ward 8 in Chicago, where Peter operated a saloon. Edith had no profession listed, but Edwin was by then working as a yard clerk for the B&O Railroad.

Peter Bateman died in 1926, leaving Edith a widow. But by 1928, she remarried, to a Carl Louis Johnson. Their marriage lasted the rest of her life, and it was happy enough for her to be described as a "beloved wife" to Carl in her obituary. If she ever spoke to her family of her time in Virginia, confessed that she'd been jailed as an accessory in a homicide, or revealed that her lover went to the gallows for murder, we cannot now know.

If she carried to her grave any guilt for her part in the death of a woman, we can know that even less.

Edith Friebel Bateman Johnson died in Chicago on September 9, 1959, at age ninety, almost certainly the last person alive who had been involved in the tragic drama of Charles and Susan Watkins.

THE MORTAL REMAINS OF Susan Wilson Watkins lie today somewhere in Salem's East Hill Cemetery North, the town's traditional African American burial place. No one will ever know the exact spot of Susan's unmarked grave—one of hundreds there—within the confines of the cemetery's two-acre lot. She has no gravestone; her name is not on the bronze plaques hung upon a memorial wall at the cemetery's entrance. When the wall was dedicated in 2005, no one yet knew her story.

In its long history, the cemetery has gone through periods of care and neglect. Too many gravestones have been toppled or lost, but today the landmark is lovingly maintained by the City of Salem. Nearby is a popular public park visited by thousands of children a month; the Salem Museum is in easy view, as is the larger, more prominent East Hill Cemetery, predominantly white. Tens of thousands of people drive by the spot along Main Street every day. But few could tell you much of the rich history that lies there, even fewer of the tragic drama of Susan Watkins.

Yet the unfortunate woman, a stranger to the community that gave her a resting place, mattered. Her name, her life, her death, forgotten for decades, should be remembered. Because her story is part of our story.

Notes

Preface

1. This account of the discovery of Susan Watkins's body is based on Lawrence Anderson's deposition in the subsequent coroner's inquest and on his testimony in the trial of Charles Watkins, as reported in the *Roanoke Times* in November 1891. That Lawrence's father, Robert Anderson, was dead is a supposition. His mother, Ann, is listed as a widow in the 1900 census, but no clear date for Robert's death has been found. He is never mentioned in the stories related to the case. The exact relationship of Lawrence to Addie Anderson, another important witness in the case also described as Watkins's cousin, is also not clear. She was perhaps an older sister.

Chapter 1. *"An Ill-Spent Life"*

2. Mark Miller, *Roanoke Valley and the Civil War: Continuity and Change* (Salem, VA: Roanoke College Center for Community Research, 1985), page 35, tables 6, 7 and 12.
3. *Conservative and Monitor* (Salem, VA), September 26, 1878. Copy in the archives of the Salem Museum.
4. Rand Dotson, Roanoke, *Virginia, 1882–1912: Magic City of the New South* (Knoxville: University of Tennessee Press, 2007), 35. In Virginia, cities

are independent of any adjacent county, while towns (like Salem at the time) share jurisdiction with their county.

5. For a description of the hanging of Stover, see *Guide to Historic Salem* 8, no. 2 (Summer 2002). For an account of the Hawley case, see *Guide to Historic Salem* 10, no. 2 (December 2004).

6. Roanoke County Appraisal Book 3, Page 401.

7. Roanoke County Will Book 1, Page 139.

8. Deedie Kagey, *When Past Is Prologue: A History of Roanoke County* (Roanoke, VA: Roanoke County Sesquicentennial Committee, 1988), 742.

9. Roanoke County Deed Book W, Page 145.

10. Ibid., 105.

Chapter 3. "At Last She Came on to Find Him"

11. This fictionalized account attempts to harmonize the testimonies of the Washingtons and Ben Wright of the first encounter between Susan and Charles in Roanoke.

12. *Roanoke Times*, January 8, 1892.

13. Roanoke County Inventory, Appraisements, and Sales Book SB 7-189, October 22, 1891, in the Roanoke County Courthouse.

14. The name of the daughter is never given in press accounts, but the 1880 census lists the names of the Wright children. Their firstborn daughter was Emma, age ten in 1880, but Emma died in 1883. Tragically, this was not the only daughter the Wrights would lose: a four-year-old girl named Willie died the following summer. So the oldest surviving daughter would seem to be Laura, about eighteen years old in 1891. All told, the Wrights seemed to have had eight children: six daughters and two sons.

Chapter 4. "A Fiendish Murder"

15. Also often spelled Cox.

16. There are occasional references in press coverage to Lawrence living with his grandmother Maria. But there is never an indication that he was at the cabin on the night Charles and Susan came by. The next afternoon, when he discovered Susan's body, he was not aware of her identity.

17. At the subsequent trial, as will be seen, a witness, Asa Jackson, would say he recalled seeing Charles and an unidentified woman that morning. But his testimony was at best uncertain.

Chapter 5. "Now a Fugitive from Justice"

18. Some of the details of John M. Oakey's business and personal history—including his unusual hobby of knitting on the streetcar—are derived from Sue Lindsey, *Oakey's Funeral Service and Crematory: The First 150 Years* (Virginia Beach, VA: Donning Company, 2016). Some other details are supposition. It stands to reason but is not provable that Richard Gholston dug Susan's grave. He was a real person employed as a gravedigger for Oakey and was indeed buried in the Oakey family plot in Salem's white cemetery in 1898. Who conducted Susan's funeral service is also not definitively known, but Pastor Benjamin Fox was the leading African American pastor in Salem and very likely officiated.

19. Roanoke County Coroner's Reports, 1891, in the Library of Virginia, Richmond, Virginia.

20. The *Roanoke Times* reported that another physician, Dr. Jacob Killian, also examined the body, but his name does not appear in the official report of the inquest.

21. Robert Thurston, *Lynching: American Mob Murder in Global Perspective* (Burlington, VT: Ashgate Publishing, 2011), 35.

Chapter 6. "Your Man Watkins in Jail Here, Awaiting Proper Papers"

22. Ben's testimony makes it clear that he could read, but I infer that Mary was not literate from the fact that she, unlike her husband, could not sign her statement made to the coroner's jury. Like several other witnesses, she signed only with an X.

23. Sometimes spelled Henning in press accounts.

24. E.A. Maccannon, *Commanders of the Dining Room: Biographic Sketches and Portraits of Successful Head Waiters* (New York: Gwendolyn Publishing House, 1904), 10.

Chapter 7. "This Is a Mighty Slow Process"

25. A.D. Smith, *Southwest Virginia and the Valley, Historical and Biographical* (Roanoke, VA: A.D. Smith and Company, 1892).
26. George Jack and E.B. Jacobs, *History of Roanoke County, History of Roanoke City and History of the Norfolk & Western Railway Company* (Roanoke, VA: Stone Printing, 1912), 54.
27. Ibid., 57–58.
28. William McCauley, *History of Roanoke County, Salem, Roanoke City, Virginia, and Representative Citizens* (Chicago: Biographical Publishing, 1902), 440.

Chapter 8. "Will He or the Jury Hang?"

29. The following July, the Roanoke County Board of Supervisors approved funds for improvements for the jail, including adding iron bars around all walls of cells. See board minutes, July 2, 1892.
30. No transcript exists of the proceedings; however, the *Roanoke Times* covered the trial extensively over the week and preserved much of the testimony. It is this coverage that was the source for the account of the trial here, usually the day after the proceedings described. The *Salem Times-Register*, a weekly, published in two successive issues a shorter synopsis of the trial, agreeing with the larger paper on most details.

Chapter 9. "Death Trap Ready"

31. Wright had seen and identified Charles's handwriting on papers in Susan's possession the previous April, before the murder. But if Ballard was aware of this fact, recorded in the coroner's inquest notes, he never sought to introduce it as evidence.
32. This was at least partially true. The physicians conducting the autopsy the previous April had described the injury to Susan's arm only as a "flesh wound," with no mention of a gunshot causing it. Understandably, the coroners concentrated primarily on the head wounds, which were the cause of death.
33. This brief synopsis is largely based on information found at www.murderbygaslight.com/2010/12/kissing-cousins.html. In a macabre twist

to the execution, a silk rope was used to hang Cluverius, ostensibly so that pieces could be cut off and sold for souvenirs. The rope stretched under his weight and did not break the condemned man's neck immediately. Instead, he strangled to death over several minutes.

34. As will be seen, there was some disagreement over the phrasing of this third point.

35. Reported, presumably verbatim, by the *Salem Times-Register* in its next issue, November 27, 1891.

Chapter 10. "The Penalty for His Brutal Crime"

36. J.A. Thomason recounted his recollections of Watkins's hanging (including the sound of a log falling) in a story in the *Salem Times-Register* on February 26, 1937. The same story described Watts Dillard's refusal to attend the event.

37. Tragedy may have haunted the Coxe family that winter. A month later, the *Roanoke Times* reported the death of a Margaret Coxe at her home west of Salem on January 5, 1892. While it could be another woman of the same name, the 1880 census records an older sister of Fannie Coxe named Margaret.

38. Norwood C. Middleton, *A Town by the Name of Salem* (Salem, VA: Salem Historical Society, 1986), 139.

39. The extra edition of the paper on the eighth had hinted that a confession had been made but gave few details.

40. No copies of these paper seem to exist, but excerpts were printed years later. The *Times-Register* quote was reprinted on August 8, 1952; the Sun excerpt appeared in the *Times-Register* on February 26, 1937.

41. Thomas Klatka, *Cultural Expressions of Nature in Sacred Contexts: Documentation of Family & Community Cemeteries in Roanoke County, Virginia* (Roanoke Regional Preservation Office, Virginia Department of Historic Resources, 2000).

Epilogue

42. "Capital Punishment in Virginia," *Virginia Law Review* 58, no. 1 (1972): 112

43. Jack and Jacobs, *History of Roanoke County*, 57–58.

44. Hu Maxwell and Howard Llewellyn Swisher, *History of Hampshire County, West Virginia: From Its Earliest Settlement to the Present* (Hampshire County, WV: A.B. Boughner, 1897), 725.

45. William McCauley, *History of Roanoke County, Salem, Roanoke City, Virginia, and Representative Citizens* (Chicago: Biographical Publishing Company, 1902), 440–41.

46. Jack and Jacobs, *History of Roanoke County*, 54–55.

47. For a solid analysis of all three of these occurrences, see Dotson, *Roanoke, Virginia, 1882–1912*, chapter 5.

48. Clare White, *Roanoke, 1740–1882* (Roanoke, VA: Roanoke Valley Historical Society, 1982), 78.

INDEX

About the Author

J ohn D. Long is the director of education at the National D-Day Memorial in Bedford, Virginia. He holds degrees from Roanoke College and the University of Virginia and has taught history at Roanoke College, Radford University and Virginia Western Community College. A contributing columnist for the *Roanoke Times*, he has also written extensively on local history and the Second World War. He and his wife, Candace, are parents of five children and live in Salem, Virginia.

Visit us at
www.historypress.com